CONFRONTING GLOBAL WARMING

Extreme
Weather

CONFRONTING GLOBAL WARMING

Extreme Weather

Tom Streissguth

Michael E. Mann
Consulting Editor

GREENHAVEN PRESS
A part of Gale, Cengage Learning

GALE
CENGAGE Learning

Detroit • New York • San Francisco • New Haven, Conn • Waterville, Maine • London

GALE
CENGAGE Learning™

Christine Nasso, *Publisher*
Elizabeth Des Chenes, *Managing Editor*

© 2011 Greenhaven Press, a part of Gale, Cengage Learning

For more information, contact:

Greenhaven Press
27500 Drake Rd.
Farmington Hills, MI 48331-3535
Or you can visit our Internet site at
gale.cengage.com.

For product information and technology assistance, contact us at
Gale Customer Support, 1-800-877-4253.

For permission to use material from this text or product, submit all requests online at
www.cengage.com/permissions.

Further permissions questions can be e-mailed to
permissionrequest@cengage.com

Every effort is made to ensure that Greenhaven Press accurately reflects the original intent of the authors. Every effort has been made to trace the owners of copyrighted material.

Cover Image © 2010 Photos.com, a division of Getty Images.

**LIBRARY OF CONGRESS
CATALOGING-IN-PUBLICATION DATA**

Streissguth, Thomas, 1958-
  Extreme weather / Tom Streissguth.
    p. cm. -- (Confronting global warming)
  Includes bibliographical references and index.
  ISBN 978-0-7377-4859-8 (hardcover)
  1. Climatic extremes. 2. Climatic changes.
  3. Weather. I. Title.
  QC981.8.C53S77 2010
  551.5--dc22
                                    2010024973

Printed in the United States of America
1 2 3 4 5 6 7 14 13 12 11 10

Contents

Preface

> "*The warnings about global warming
> have been extremely clear for a long
> time. We are facing a global climate
> crisis. It is deepening. We are entering
> a period of consequences.*"
>
> *Al Gore*

Still hotly debated by some, human-induced global warming
is now accepted in the scientific community. Earth's average
yearly temperature is getting steadily warmer; sea levels are rising
due to melting ice caps; and the resulting impact on ocean life,
wildlife, and human life is already evident. The human-induced
buildup of greenhouse gases in the atmosphere poses serious and
diverse threats to life on earth. As scientists work to develop accurate models to predict the future impact of global warming,
researchers, policy makers, and industry leaders are coming to
terms with what can be done today to halt and reverse the human
contributions to global climate change.

Each volume in the Confronting Global Warming series ex-
amines the current and impending challenges the planet faces
because of global warming. Several titles focus on a particular
aspect of life—such as weather, farming, health, or nature and
wildlife—that has been altered by climate change. Consulting the
works of leading experts in the field, Confronting Global Warming authors present the current status of those aspects as they
have been affected by global warming, highlight key future challenges, examine potential solutions for dealing with the results
of climate change, and address the pros and cons of imminent
changes and challenges. Other volumes in the series—such as
those dedicated to the role of government, the role of industry,
and the role of the individual—address the impact various fac-

ets of society can have on climate change. The result is a series that provides students and general-interest readers with a solid understanding of the worldwide ramifications of climate change and what can be done to help humanity adapt to changing conditions and mitigate damage.

Each volume includes:

- A descriptive **table of contents** listing subtopics, charts, graphs, maps, and sidebars included in each chapter
- Full-color **charts, graphs, and maps** to illustrate key points, concepts, and theories
- Full-color **photos** that enhance textual material
- **Sidebars** that provide explanations of technical concepts or statistical information, present case studies to illustrate the international impact of global warming, or offer excerpts from primary and secondary documents
- **Pulled quotes** containing key points and statistical figures
- A **glossary** providing users with definitions of important terms
- An annotated **bibliography** of additional books, periodicals, and Web sites for further research
- A detailed **subject index** to allow users to quickly find the information they need

The Confronting Global Warming series provides students and general-interest readers with the information they need to understand the complex issue of climate change. Titles in the series offer users a well-rounded view of global warming, presented in an engaging format. Confronting Global Warming not only provides context for how society has dealt with climate change thus far but also encapsulates debates about how it will confront issues related to climate in the future.

Foreword

Earth's climate is a complex system of interacting natural components. These components include the atmosphere, the ocean, and the continental ice sheets. Living things on earth—or, the biosphere—also constitute an important component of the climate system.

Natural Factors Cause Some of Earth's Warming and Cooling

Numerous factors influence Earth's climate system, some of them natural. For example, the slow drift of continents that takes place over millions of years, a process known as plate tectonics, influences the composition of the atmosphere through its impact on volcanic activity and surface erosion. Another significant factor involves naturally occurring gases in the atmosphere, known as greenhouse gases, which have a warming influence on Earth's surface. Scientists have known about this warming effect for nearly two centuries: These gases absorb outgoing heat energy and direct it back toward the surface. In the absence of this natural greenhouse effect, Earth would be a frozen, and most likely lifeless, planet.

Another natural factor affecting Earth's climate—this one measured on timescales of several millennia—involves cyclical variations in the geometry of Earth's orbit around the sun. These variations alter the distribution of solar radiation over the surface of Earth and are responsible for the coming and going of the ice ages every 100,000 years or so. In addition, small variations in the brightness of the sun drive minor changes in Earth's surface temperature over decades and centuries. Explosive volcanic activity, such as the Mount Pinatubo eruption in the Philippines in 1991, also affects Earth's climate. These eruptions inject highly reflective particles called aerosol into the upper part of the atmosphere, known as the stratosphere, where they can reside for a year or longer. These particles reflect some of the incoming sunlight back into space and cool Earth's surface for years at a time.

Human Progress Puts Pressure on Natural Climate Patterns

Since the dawn of the industrial revolution some two centuries ago, however, humans have become the principal drivers of climate change. The burning of fossil fuels—such as oil, coal, and natural gas—has led to an increase in atmospheric levels of carbon dioxide, a powerful greenhouse gas. And farming practices have led to increased atmospheric levels of methane, another potent greenhouse gas. If humanity continues such activities at the current rate through the end of this century, the concentrations of greenhouse gases in the atmosphere will be higher than they have been for tens of millions of years. It is the unprecedented rate at which we are amplifying the greenhouse effect, warming Earth's surface, and modifying our climate that causes scientists so much concern.

The Role of Scientists in Climate Observation and Projection

Scientists study Earth's climate not just from observation but also from a theoretical perspective. Modern-day climate models successfully reproduce the key features of Earth's climate, including the variations in wind patterns around the globe, the major ocean current systems such as the Gulf Stream, and the seasonal changes in temperature and rainfall associated with Earth's annual revolution around the sun. The models also reproduce some of the more complex natural oscillations of the climate system. Just as the atmosphere displays random day-to-day variability that we term "weather," the climate system produces its own random variations, on timescales of years. One important example is the phenomenon called El Niño, a periodic warming of the eastern tropical Pacific Ocean surface that influences seasonal patterns of temperature and rainfall around the globe. The ability to use models to reproduce the climate's complicated natural oscillatory behavior gives scientists increased confidence that these models are up to the task of mimicking the climate system's response to human impacts.

To that end, scientists have subjected climate models to a number of rigorous tests of their reliability. James Hansen of the NASA Goddard Institute for Space Studies performed a famous experiment back in 1988, when he subjected a climate model (one relatively primitive by modern standards) to possible future fossil fuel emissions scenarios. For the scenario that most closely matches actual emissions since then, the model's predicted course of global temperature increase shows an uncanny correspondence to the actual increase in temperature over the intervening two decades. When Mount Pinatubo erupted in the Philippines in 1991, Hansen performed another famous experiment. Before the volcanic aerosol had an opportunity to influence the climate (it takes several months to spread globally throughout the atmosphere), he took the same climate model and subjected it to the estimated atmospheric aerosol distribution. Over the next two years, actual global average surface temperatures proceeded to cool a little less than 1°C (1.8°F), just as Hansen's model predicted they would.

Given that there is good reason to trust the models, scientists can use them to answer important questions about climate change. One such question weighs the human factors against the natural factors to determine responsibility for the dramatic changes currently taking place in our climate. When driven by natural factors alone, climate models do not reproduce the observed warming of the past century. Only when these models are also driven by human factors—primarily, the increase in greenhouse gas concentrations—do they reproduce the observed warming. Of course, the models are not used just to look at the past. To make projections of future climate change, climate scientists consider various possible scenarios or pathways of future human activity. The earth has warmed roughly 1°C since preindustrial times. In the "business as usual" scenario, where we continue the current course of burning fossil fuel through the twenty-first century, models predict an additional warming anywhere from roughly 2°C to 5°C (3.6°F to 9°F). The models also show that even if we were to stop fossil fuel burning today, we are probably committed to as much as 0.6°C additional warming because of the inertia of the climate system. This inertia ensures warming for a century to come, simply due to our greenhouse gas emissions thus far. This committed warming introduces a profound procrastination penalty for not taking immediate action. If we are to avert an additional warming of 1°C, which would bring the net warming to 2°C—often considered an appropriate threshold for defining dangerous human impact on our climate—we have to act almost immediately.

Long-Term Warming May Bring About Extreme Changes Worldwide

In the "business as usual" emissions scenario, climate change will have an array of substantial impacts on our society and the environment by the end of this century. Patterns of rainfall and drought are projected to shift in such a way that some regions currently stressed for water resources, such as the desert southwest of the United States and the Middle East, are likely to become drier. More intense rainfall events in other regions, such as Europe and the midwestern United States, could lead to increased flooding. Heat waves like the one in Europe in summer 2003, which killed more than 30,000 people, are projected to become far more common. Atlantic hurricanes are likely to reach greater intensities, potentially doing far more damage to coastal infrastructure.

Furthermore, regions such as the Arctic are expected to warm faster than the rest of the globe. Disappearing Arctic sea ice already threatens wildlife, including polar bears and walruses. Given another 2°C warming (3.6°F), a substantial portion of the Greenland ice sheet is likely to melt. This event, combined with other factors, could lead to more than 1 meter (about 3 feet) of sea-level rise by the end of the century. Such a rise in sea level would threaten many American East Coast and Gulf Coast cities, as well as low-lying coastal regions and islands around the world. Food production in tropical regions, already insufficient to meet the needs of some populations, will probably decrease with future warming. The incidence of infectious disease is expected to increase in higher elevations and in latitudes with warming temperatures. In short, the impacts of future climate change are likely to have a devastating impact on society and our environment in the absence of intervention.

Strategies for Confronting Climate Change

Options for dealing with the threats of climate change include both adaptation to inevitable changes and mitigation, or lessening, of those changes that we can still affect. One possible adaptation would be to adjust our agricultural practices to the changing regional patterns of temperature and rainfall. Another would be to build coastal defenses against the inundation from sea-level rise. Only mitigation, however, can prevent the most threatening changes. One means of mitigation that has been given much recent attention is geoengineering. This method involves perturbing the climate system in such a way as to partly or fully offset the warming impact of rising greenhouse gas concentrations. One geoengineering approach involves periodically shooting aerosol particles, similar to ones produced by volcanic eruptions, into the stratosphere—essentially emulating the cooling impact of a major volcanic eruption on an ongoing basis. As with nearly all geoengineering proposals, there are potential perils with this scheme, including an increased tendency for continental drought and the acceleration of stratospheric ozone depletion.

The only foolproof strategy for climate change mitigation is the decrease of greenhouse gas emissions. If we are to avert a dangerous 2°C increase relative to preindustrial times, we will probably need to bring greenhouse gas emissions to a peak within the coming years and reduce them well below current levels within the coming decades. Any strategy for such a reduction of emissions must be international and multipronged, involving greater conservation of energy resources; a shift toward alternative, carbon-free sources of energy; and a coordinated set of governmental policies that encourage responsible corporate and individual practices. Some contrarian voices argue that we cannot afford to take such steps. Actually, given the procrastination penalty of not acting on the climate change problem, what we truly cannot afford is to delay action.

Evidently, the problem of climate change crosses multiple disciplinary boundaries and involves the physical, biological, and social sciences. As an issue facing all of civilization, climate change demands political, economic, and ethical considerations. With the Confronting Global Warming series, Greenhaven Press addresses all of these considerations in an accessible format. In ten thorough volumes, the series covers the full range of climate change impacts (water and ice; extreme weather; population, resources, and conflict; nature and wildlife; farming and food supply; health and disease) and the various essential components of any solution to the climate change problem (energy production and alternative energy; the role of government; the role of industry; and the role of the individual). It is my hope and expectation that this series will become a useful resource for anyone who is curious about not only the nature of the problem but also about what we can do to solve it.

Michael E. Mann

Michael E. Mann is a professor in the Department of Meteorology at Penn State University and director of the Penn State Earth

System Science Center. In 2002 he was selected as one of the fifty leading visionaries in science and technology by Scientific American. *He was a lead author for the "Observed Climate Variability and Change" chapter of the Intergovernmental Panel on Climate Change (IPCC) Third Scientific Assessment Report, and in 2007 he shared the Nobel Peace Prize with other IPCC authors. He is the author of more than 120 peer-reviewed publications, and he recently coauthored the book* Dire Predictions: Understanding Global Warming *with colleague Lee Kump. Mann is also a co-founder and avid contributor to the award-winning science Web site RealClimate.org.*

CHAPTER 1

Global Climate Change and Extreme Weather: An Introduction

The global climate includes many different natural elements, including temperature, humidity, precipitation, barometric pressure, and wind. These elements vary over time and by location. Each region of the earth has its particular climate, which varies with latitude, elevation, local terrain, and proximity to the sea and other large bodies of water. On a global scale, climate is also affected by the earth's rotation, solar radiation, and the chemical makeup of the atmosphere.

Scientists measure climate by averaging temperature and other statistics over a period of time. They also gauge climate extremes by examining the range of particular variables. For example, the highest and lowest temperature experienced over a given period of time shows the temperature range. This range varies, as does the number of extreme days, defined as those days when the temperature reaches within 10 percent of its historic high or low.

Weather is the local experience of climatic elements. In any location, weather varies from day to day, and sometimes changes drastically in the course of a day. Weather is hard to predict, although meteorologists have made it their profession to understand exactly how it changes from day to day. People living in a certain location know, most of the time, what to expect. On some days, extreme and unexpected weather strikes. Extreme weather can drastically affect the way people live and the well-being of their homes and families.

Until recently, meteorologists understood extreme weather as a natural phenomenon, caused by an unusual combination of natural variables such as wind, temperature, and pressure. But the changing chemical makeup of the atmosphere, caused by human activity, may be having an effect on the global climate and giving rise to anthropogenic (human-caused) extreme weather. Although the costs to address and solve global warming may be high, the costs of doing nothing may be high as well. Between 1980 and 2004, the United States has undergone fifty-eight weather-related disasters that caused damages of $1 billion or more, and these extreme weather events are happening more often.[1]

Air and Water Chemistry

Earth's atmosphere extends about 75 miles (121 km) into space from sea level. It is made up of various gases, including 78 percent nitrogen, 21 percent oxygen, and 1 percent argon. There are small amounts of trace gases as well, including carbon dioxide, methane, ozone, and water vapor. Human activity has added pollutants such as sulfur dioxide and mercury to the atmosphere, and has also increased the concentration of natural compounds such as carbon dioxide.

The chemistry of Earth's atmosphere has important effects on climate. The atmosphere absorbs ultraviolet rays and other forms of harmful radiation emitted by the sun. Some of the solar radiation that penetrates the atmosphere is trapped before it can return to space. This natural greenhouse effect helps to maintain a fairly constant ground temperature, allowing life to flourish.

Oceans cover about two-thirds of the planet's surface. The chemistry of the ocean is affected by the changing composition of the atmosphere; most importantly, seawater naturally absorbs compounds such as carbon dioxide, which increases oceanic acidity. Measured on the pH scale, the present acidity of the ocean is about 8.05. This value represents a fall from a pH of 8.2 in previous centuries (as the pH measure drops, acidity increases). In addition, the average sea-surface and underwater temperatures of the ocean are rising.

In a warming aquatic environment with a changing chemical balance, many organisms lose their ability to thrive under the surface. As seawater warms, for example, the algae that attaches to underwater coral reefs detaches itself from the coral. This process starves coral of needed nutrients, a process that bleaches it (turns it white). Dying coral reefs leave many coastlines without an important defense against storm surges that occur during hurricanes.

Components of Earth's Climate

There are several important components of the earth's climate. Scientists measure these components to assess and predict the weather. The measurements are affected by conditions in the atmosphere, including atmospheric chemistry, as well as local conditions and topography.

Humidity Humidity is the concentration of water vapor in the atmosphere; relative humidity is the amount of water vapor expressed as a percentage. At 100 percent relative humidity, the air is saturated with water vapor. At 0 percent, water vapor is absent.

Barometric Pressure Barometric pressure is the weight of the atmosphere over a given point, measured in millibars, which equal roughly a thousandth of the atmospheric pressure at sea level. Air flows from an area of high pressure to one of lower pressure. As a result, pressure gradients (changes) cause the movement of air—wind. When very low pressure occurs, high winds are a result.

Temperature Temperature is a measure of the movement or energy of atoms within any substance. The higher the energy, the warmer the gas, solid, or liquid. The temperature of the atmosphere is an important measure of weather conditions. Heat naturally flows between two areas of different temperature. In addition, warm air tends to rise, while cold air falls. Warm air also has a greater capacity to hold water vapor. Ground temperature is affected by the amount of solar radiation received at the earth's surface, and by the amount of such radiation that is trapped through the greenhouse effect.

Precipitation Precipitation is the condensation of water vapor in the atmosphere and its fall to the earth in various forms, including rain, snow, and hail. Condensation increases as temperature falls or as water vapor is added to the atmosphere. In the water cycle, the evaporation of water from the ocean increases the concentration of water vapor in the air. The water vapor rises, forms clouds, condenses, and falls back to the earth. Depending on topography and other conditions, different regions of the earth receive varying amounts, and forms, of precipitation—all in the fairly predictable pattern of local climate.

Solar Radiation and Global Climate

The sun is an enormous nuclear furnace, burning 700 million tons of hydrogen each second, converting that hydrogen to helium, and emitting radiation (partly in the form of visible light) that takes eight minutes to reach Earth. The sun also emits an enormous amount of invisible energy in the form of X rays, gamma rays, and ultraviolet radiation.

The energy put out by the sun—the basic fuel of the global climate system—varies over time. One important factor affecting this energy level is the occurrence of sunspots, large magnetic storms on the surface of the sun. Sunspots occur in cycles of about 11 years (longer sunspot cycles take place in cycles of 90 years and 180 years). Sunspots reduce the surface temperature of the sun. Magnetic activity increases during high sunspot activity, however, compensating for the loss of radiated energy.

About 40 percent of the solar energy received at the top of Earth's atmosphere eventually reaches the surface of the planet. Harmful X rays and gamma rays are taken up by oxygen and nitrogen in the atmosphere and converted to heat. Most of the harmful ultraviolet radiation is absorbed by a layer of atmospheric ozone. On average, about 30 percent of solar radiation that arrives at the earth is reflected, by the ground and the atmosphere, back into space.

Variations in solar output may affect Earth's global climate. But scientists have been making accurate and detailed data on solar radiation only for about 30 years. From this limited range, conclusions about the links between solar energy and climate variance on Earth are still uncertain and the subject of scientific debate.

The Milankovitch Cycles and Global Climate

The earth's movement and position have important effects on global climate. As the earth rotates around the sun, the planet's current 23.5-degree tilt to the plane of its orbit causes the seasons. During summer in the northern hemisphere, the northern half of the planet is tilted toward the sun. Receiving more sunlight, the north has warmer weather and rain. During winter, this half points away from the sun, bringing colder weather as well as snow.

Over long periods of time, the earth shifts position as it rotates, slowly changing its orbital tilt between 22.5 degrees and 24.5 degrees. This obliquity, as it is known, occurs over a span of forty-one thousand orbits of the sun (years). When the tilt is at its highest—that is, most acute—summers and winters are more severe. When the tilt is least acute, the seasons are less severe.

Another cycle is known as the precession of the equinoxes. This arises from the fact that the earth wobbles like a spinning top on its vertical axis. As the globe wobbles, this axis traces out a circular pattern over a period of twenty-six thounsand years.

Precession gradually shifts the position of the planet and changes the amount of solar radiation that reaches its surface.

The slightly oval shape of Earth's orbit also has an effect. As it moves through this orbit, the planet gets closer to the sun, then it moves farther away. Earth's average distance from the sun is 93 million miles. At perihelion, Earth reaches its closest point to the sun; at aphelion, the planet is about 4 million miles farther away. The perihelion and aphelion points shift slowly over a period of twenty-two thousand years. At present, perihelion occurs in January, when the northern hemisphere is tilted away from the sun. This raises northern hemisphere winter temperatures. When perihelion occurs in July, during the northern hemisphere's summer, the hot season is even hotter, the cold season colder, and weather around the world more extreme.

Another cycle occurs as the earth's orbit slowly changes its shape, from oval to nearly circular and back again. This eccentricity, as such deviation is called, changes gradually over a period of about 100,000 years. At present, it causes a variation of about 7 percent in the intensity of solar radiation received by the earth at perihelion versus at aphelion. This difference can reach a maximum of 20 percent when the earth follows a more eccentric (oblong) orbit.

It was the theory of Milutin Milankovitch, an early twentieth-century astronomer, that all of these cycles—eccentricity, precession, and obliquity—significantly affect the amount of solar radiation received on Earth. According to this idea, the Milankovitch cycles, as they are known today, have an impact on global climate and are responsible for the gradual warming and cooling of Earth over long periods of time. Milankovitch proposed these cycles as an explanation of a puzzling phenomenon, one that still divides scientists: the ice ages.

Following pages: Carbon emissions from coal-fired power plants contribute to air pollution in cities such as Linfen, China, one of the most polluted cities in the world. Peter Parks/AFP/ Getty Images.

The Ice Ages

The earth has been through long periods of global cooling known as the ice ages (or glacial ages). The most recent ice age ended about ten thousand years ago. During an ice age, the mean surface temperature on Earth drops significantly. Glaciers expand, and ice sheets spread across the continents from the polar regions.

During an ice age, the surface cover of ice and snow increases the albedo, or reflectivity, of the earth. As more solar radiation is reflected back into space, the heat energy reaching the surface decreases. A feedback loop (a self-reinforcing phenomenon) occurs, steadily lowering temperatures and extending the surface glaciation. For this reason, periods of extensive glaciation last much longer than interglacial periods, such as the current Holocene epoch.

Scientists are still debating the causes of the ice ages. There may be several factors at work, including Milankovitch cycles and the circulation and temperature of the water in the ocean. Variances in the amount of energy emitted by the sun may also be at work. Another factor may be a change in the chemical composition of the atmosphere that causes the level of carbon dioxide to fall, which traps incoming solar radiation.

The Medieval Warm Period and the Little Ice Age

Average temperatures can fluctuate over decades and centuries. Within the present interglacial phase, there have been several periods of rising or falling temperatures. The Medieval Warm Period, which lasted from the ninth to the thirteenth centuries, brought higher average temperatures to Europe and the North Atlantic Ocean. During this period, the Vikings traveled from Scandinavia to settle in Greenland and Newfoundland, encouraged by more temperate winters and the retreat of sea ice from the North Atlantic.

The Medieval Warm Period was followed by the Little Ice Age, which began in the sixteenth century. Temperatures fell throughout Europe and in North America. Unable to survive the more severe winters, the Greenland colonies died out. Glaciers advanced to lower elevations throughout Europe. The Thames River in London, the rivers of northern Europe, and New York harbor froze solid during the winters. By the middle of the nineteenth century, temperatures were rising again.

Scientists still disagree on the true nature of the Medieval Warm Period and the Little Ice Age. These climate phases might not be examples of global warming and cooling. Instead, they may represent fluctuations in regional climate systems. Although other parts of the world have also experienced warming and cooling trends, timing and intensity vary greatly from one location to the next. If these phases were examples of global climate change, they may be analogous to the global warming that is presently occurring. They lacked only one factor: the rise of greenhouse gases, added to the atmosphere by industrialized human societies.

Measuring Carbon Dioxide

To measure change in global climate, scientists need statistics for present conditions and for past years. They need accurate measurements of temperature, precipitation levels, and humidity. But data series do not run back very long. The first annual rainfall measurements were taken in the middle of the nineteenth century. A little more than 100 years ago, observers began taking regular temperature readings in scattered locations around the world. To make up for the shortfall in data, scientists have developed data from farming records, from the varying thickness of tree rings, from examining ocean sediments, and by a chemical analysis of cores drilled out of glaciers and polar ice.

To understand Earth's gradual warming, another valuable data set measures the level of greenhouse gases, including carbon dioxide (CO_2), which has always been present in the atmosphere. Scientists have been able to measure its historic concentration by

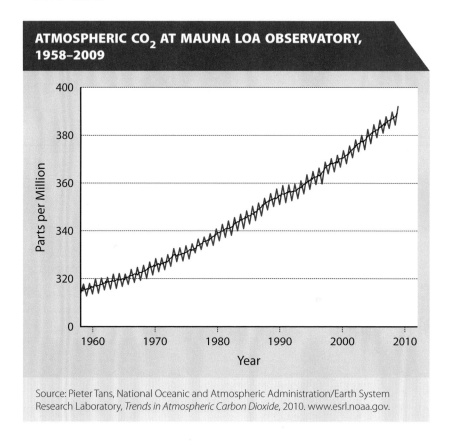

ATMOSPHERIC CO$_2$ AT MAUNA LOA OBSERVATORY, 1958–2009

Parts per Million

Year

Source: Pieter Tans, National Oceanic and Atmospheric Administration/Earth System Research Laboratory, *Trends in Atmospheric Carbon Dioxide*, 2010. www.esrl.noaa.gov.

analyzing ice cores. They have discovered that before the industrial age that began in the eighteenth century, the atmosphere averaged about 280 parts per million (ppm) of carbon dioxide molecules.

Several weather theorists believed that rising carbon dioxide might bring a rise in temperatures. In 1958, an American scientist, Charles Keeling, installed CO$_2$ measuring instruments on the slopes of Mauna Loa, a volcanic mountain in Hawaii. Since that time, these instruments have documented a natural, annual fluctuation of carbon dioxide levels. During the warm months in the northern hemisphere, the intake of CO$_2$ by plants reduces the level of this compound in the atmosphere. In the winter, with plants dormant, CO$_2$ levels naturally increase.

Since the late 1950s, scientists at the Mauna Loa Observatory in Hawaii have tracked the average level of carbon dioxide in the atmosphere—and seen it rise. AP Images.

The "Keeling Curve" documents another fact: a steady rise in the average level of carbon dioxide. The instruments on Mauna Loa first showed a level of 315 ppm. By 2000, Keeling's measurement had reached 367 ppm; the measurement rose to 385 ppm in 2008.

There are many human-induced, or anthropogenic, factors contributing to this increase. The burning of coal to generate steam power for industries began two hundred years ago. Beginning in the early twentieth century, crude oil, refined into gasoline, powered millions of vehicles. Agriculture also makes an impact on CO_2 levels. The burning of forests to clear land for pasture or crops releases large amounts of CO_2. The use of chemical fertilizers emits nitrous oxide, and livestock contribute the greenhouse gas methane through their digestion. The cultivation of rice on flooded plains also releases large amounts of methane into the atmosphere.

Anthropogenic Climate Change

The issue of anthropogenic climate change has become a major topic of scientific study, one that is an almost daily topic of news reports. Climate research now engages thousands of scientists working at public agencies, research institutes, universities, and weather bureaus. To coordinate the findings of this global research, the United Nations established the Intergovernmental Panel on Climate Change (IPCC) in 1988. This body is made up of hundreds of scientists, whose job is to review data, carry out research, and summarize their findings in reports. From time to time, the IPCC releases an assessment report on climate change. These reports have become a vital information source for anyone studying the problem of global warming.

The IPCC's latest report, from 2007, found that the phenomenon of global warming is unequivocal, and that the earth's average temperature rose by 1.3°F (.74°C) from 1906 to 2005. In addition, the IPCC found that human activity was very likely the source of this warming, and chances of it being the result of entirely natural processes was less than 5 percent. According to the report, carbon dioxide emissions increased 70 percent between 1970 and 2004, and they are rising at a steadily faster rate. From 1990 through 1999, emissions rose by 1 percent; from 2000 through 2004, by 3 percent. The report projected further melting of the polar ice caps, sea-level rise through the twenty-first century, and a better than 90 percent chance of more frequent heat waves and heavy rainfall.

Also in 2007, the American Meteorological Society weighed in with an information statement. The AMS also recognized a rise in global temperatures, and explained that:

"In recent decades, humans have increasingly affected local, regional, and global climate by altering the flows of radiative energy and water . . . Indeed, strong observational evidence and results from modeling studies indicate that, at least over the last 50 years, human activities are a major contributor to climate change."[2]

Scientific reports on climate change mention, as one of several impacts, an increase in the occurrence of extreme weather: events such as storms, floods, and droughts that are expected to have less than a 10 percent chance of occurring in any one place. Through feedback loops and the indirect effects of distant phenomena, even small changes in normal weather patterns can bring about extreme climate. But because scientists have such a limited set of historic data on which to base their projections, the rate of increase in extreme weather remains uncertain. Projections of future climate impacts also remind readers that no specific weather event can be linked to the phenomenon of global warming.

The Climate Extremes Index

Nevertheless, the National Climatic Data Center (NCDC) is making the attempt to quantify the change in extreme weather in the United States. Using data from more than one thousand weather stations throughout the country, NCDC scientists have developed a Climate Extremes Index (CEI) to measure three variables: temperature, precipitation, and drought severity. The index expresses climate extreme as a percentage of the country experiencing extreme readings (defined as readings lying at the upper or lower 10 percent of the current range). The larger the area experiencing extreme readings, the higher the index.

Based on readings of the Climate Extremes Index, the area of the United States experiencing extreme weather has been rising since the 1970s. The increase has been taking place largely in the summer; five of the fifteen most extreme years have taken place since 1997, with 1998 holding the record as the most extreme year (1934 runs second). There were shorter periods of high CEI values in the 1930s and 1950s, when the country experienced drought and high temperatures.

2008 — An Exception to the Trend?

A shift in the temperature of ocean currents across the Pacific occurred in late 2007, lowering average global temperatures in

Climatologists Battle: Kerry Emanuel Versus Bill Gray

For all its cold calculation and studies in fact and reason, climatology—like many other scientific fields—has its share of lively debate, emotional disagreements, and bitter rivalries. In the battle over global warming science, one main bout is taking place between Kerry Emanuel, a researcher at the Massachusetts Institute of Technology, and William Gray, a hurricane forecaster at Colorado State University. Emanuel went through a conversion from global-warming skepticism after releasing a study of the effect of warming sea-surface temperatures on the intensity of tropical cyclones—a paper published in the summer of 2005, just three weeks before the devastating Hurricane Katrina made landfall on the Gulf of Mexico coastline. Gray, on the other hand, remains a convinced global-warming skeptic. Widely respected for his ability to predict hurricane frequency, Gray has no hesitation in expressing his doubts about global-warming science and about the motivation of those who believe the climate is undergoing a drastic, anthropogenic change.

2008 to 57.76°F (14.31°C). Unusually heavy snowfalls took place in the western United States and Canada. They gave global warming skeptics an opportunity to assert that anthropogenic climate change was either having less effect than previously thought or was untrue altogether. Despite the cooling trend, however, 2008 was still the tenth warmest year on record for global temperatures in the last century and a half.

Not all extreme weather depends on a rise in global average temperatures. In the cool year of 2008, several deadly tropical storms made landfall in the southern United States and the Caribbean. Strong tropical storms developed in the western Pacific, while unusually severe drought persisted in Australia and many other regions of the world. Extreme cold in central Asia and China disrupted harvests and transportation systems. In the

In a statement to the U.S. Senate on September 28, 2005, Gray concisely laid out his opinion that "this topic has long ago advanced into the political arena and taken on a life of its own. It has been extended and grossly exaggerated and misused by those wishing to make gains from the exploitation of ignorance on this subject . . . It is unfortunate that most of the resources for climate research come from the federal government. When a national government takes a political position on a scientific topic, the wise meteorologist or climatologist either joins the crowd or keeps his/her mouth shut. Scientists can be punished if they do not accept the current views of their funding agents. An honest and objective scientific debate cannot be held in such a political environment."

In 2008, Emanuel himself took a "modified" stand on the question of the global warming–hurricane link. Using a new computer model, he ran seven different simulations in an attempt to project the total number and intensity of hurricanes in two centuries. In two of the simulations, he found a decline in overall intensity; in five simulations, a small increase. "The take-home message is that we've got a lot of work to do," he reported in an April 12, 2008 *Houston Chronicle* article. "There's still a lot of uncertainty in this problem."

Bay of Bengal, Cyclone Nargis struck Myanmar, causing as many as one hundred thousand deaths.

Disruptive hurricanes, floods, droughts, and heat waves will affect the ability of poorer nations to supply food and other essential goods to their populations.

Extreme Weather: The Future Impact

If extreme weather worsens and becomes more commonplace, there will be severe future social, economic, and political effects. Disruptive hurricanes, floods, droughts, and heat waves will affect the ability of poorer nations to supply food and other essential goods to their populations. As a result, those people will become more dependent on aid agencies and foreign donors for these goods, and rivalry over dwindling natural resources—fertile soil, energy, and water—will spark political and military conflict around the globe.

Migration from affected areas could also occur, as farmers and rural people unable to support their families migrate to urban areas to improve their chances of survival. Already overburdened cities could be overwhelmed by this migration and find themselves hard pressed to supply food, water, housing, medical care, and security to their residents.

Wealthier societies will be better equipped to adapt to a changing climate and environment. The cost will burden their economies, however, and more occurrences of extreme weather will bring a general rise in prices and a decline in living standards. Since 2005, the prices of basic foods such as wheat, rice, corn, and milk have been increasing around the world. Many observers also believe that an era of peak oil has been reached, and that falling stocks of this energy resource are now driving its price upward. The spike in oil prices has come at a time when economies around the world have sunk into recession and a credit crisis is threatening the collapse of the global financial system.

An era of economic troubles has begun just as the damage caused by extreme weather is increasing. The two events may be closely linked. In their book *Climate Code Red: The Case for Emergency Action*, David Spratt and Philip Sutton write that "It seems that the price of food . . . is becoming a key indicator of a new phenomenon: a multi-issue crisis of sustainability that incorporates food, water, peak oil, and global warming. At the same time, the natural physical infrastructure on which all living things depend is being put under more and more stress . . . Since the beginning of the industrial revolution, we have failed to build and maintain a system that has enabled modern society to ensure its own sustainability and that of other living species."[3]

Notes

1. Paul Douglas, *Restless Skies: The Ultimate Weather Book*. New York: Sterling, 2007, p. 8.
2. "Climate Change: An Information Statement of the American Meteorological Society," *Bulletin of the American Meteorological Society*, February 2007. www.ametsoc .org.
3. David Spratt and Philip Sutton, *Climate Code Red: The Case for Emergency Action*. Melbourne, Australia: Scribe, 2008, pp. 150–151.

Chapter 2

Heat Waves

The Great Plains didn't offer much to the American settlers of the nineteenth century. The land was flat and featureless, and covered by useless prairie grasses. There were few natural water sources, and there was very little timber for building houses, barns, and fences. Many western emigrants pushed on, over the Rocky Mountains to the Pacific coast, where farming conditions were far better.

The Homestead Act of 1862 changed that view. This new law granted 160 acres of land free to anyone who would settle and farm it. A land rush occurred in the Midwest as thousands of families moved to the prairies. They broke the sod, raised homes, planted crops, and marked off pastures. A long period of favorable weather encouraged them in the mistaken belief that "rain follows the plow"—that preparing the land for farming also improves the weather for raising crops and livestock.

Things changed for the worse in the 1930s. A severe drought destroyed millions of acres of crops. By not rotating their crops, farmers had exhausted the topsoil, which plowing had left exposed to wind and erosion. Windstorms blew eastward across the prairies, gathering huge, black clouds of dust and dirt that reached heights of 16,000 feet in some places. From 1930 through 1936, a series of killer heat waves brought temperatures of 120°F to 125°F (48.9°C to 51.67°C) to areas of the Great Plains and caused fifteen thousand heat-related deaths.[1] These Dust Bowl years were the hottest, driest years in U.S. history.

Since the Dust Bowl, the number and intensity of heat waves has been increasing. A heat wave comparable to that of 1936 struck the central United States in 1983. Another heat wave and drought struck the same region in 1988. Temperatures climbed well over 100°F (37.78°C) on several occasions in the Northeast in 1999. In all these periods of higher-than-average temperatures, people died from heat stroke and heat exhaustion. According to a study group known as the Heat Wave Awareness Project, "Although [heat waves] are far less property-destructive than other extreme weather events, more lives have been claimed over the past fifteen years by heat than by all other extreme weather events combined . . . "[2]

Rising Temperatures

Temperature is the most thoroughly measured climate statistic available, with readings in the United States going back about 150 years. With this long and reliable data set, scientists can determine median and average temperatures over a long period of time. They can also draw on very precise, localized statistics that allow them to measure climate change on a regional scale.

"Although [heat waves] are far less property-destructive than other extreme weather events, more lives have been claimed over the past fifteen years by heat than by all other extreme weather events combined."

These records testify that the global average surface temperature rose about .9°F (.5°C) between the 1880s and 1970s. Since the mid-1970s, the average surface temperature has risen an additional 1°F (.55°C), and continues to rise at a rate of about 2.9°F (1.61°C) per century. The warmest year on record, 2005, took place during a warm stretch that goes back to 2000, and in which eight of the warmest years in the last 120 years have all taken place.[3]

Despite the cool year of 2008 in much of North America, global average temperatures continue to rise, both on land and at sea. The coolest year of the twenty-first century, 2008 was still the ninth warmest year on record since 1880.[4]

In June 2009, the National Oceanic and Atmospheric Administration (NOAA) measured the second warmest month on record. The combined land and sea surface temperatures were the warmest on record (.11°F warmer than the previous record, set in 2005). The average ocean temperature reached 62.6°F (17°C), the warmest measure in 130 years of data.

The average ocean temperature is a more comprehensive measure of the planet's rising temperature, as the seas tend to warm more gradually than the land and retain their warmth for a longer period of time. NOAA blamed recent increases on anthropogenic global warming along with the El Niño phenomenon, a warm Pacific Ocean current that returned to the coast of South America in 2009 and warmed the air over the rest of the hemisphere.[5]

Average minimum temperatures are rising as well; in fact, the average low temperature in the United States is rising faster than the average high. There have been rising minimum temperatures at night, which worsens the impact of heat waves. But the rising minimums bring a fall in the number of frost days (and freezing nights), which benefit farmers by killing insect pests and diseases that harm crops. In 2004, a study by the National Center for Atmospheric Research found that, as the jet stream shifts and pulls warmer air over coastal regions, the number of frost days will drop most significantly in western North America and northwest Europe.[6]

The warming trend is strongest in Alaska and the western United States. The number of unusually cold days and nights is falling; the number of days of frost is falling; and the frost-free season is lengthening. In addition, average temperatures in the troposphere, the atmospheric layer that reaches nine miles above the surface, are also rising. The troposphere itself is expanding, at its fastest rate in tropical regions. According to a 2003 study by Benjamin Santer and colleagues at the U.S. Lawrence Livermore National Laboratory, the average depth of the troposphere

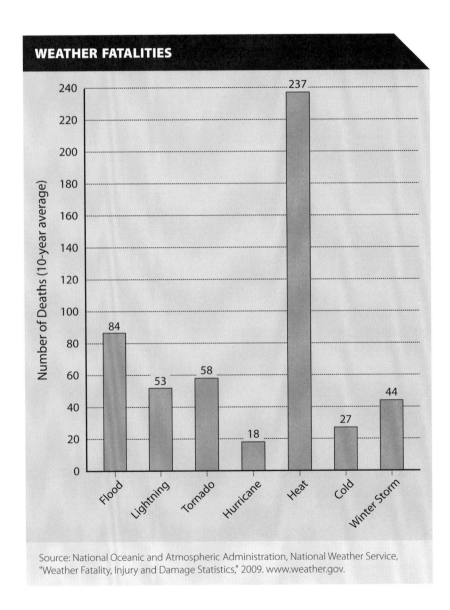

WEATHER FATALITIES

Number of Deaths (10-year average)

Flood	Lightning	Tornado	Hurricane	Heat	Cold	Winter Storm
84	53	58	18	237	27	44

Source: National Oceanic and Atmospheric Administration, National Weather Service, "Weather Fatality, Injury and Damage Statistics," 2009. www.weather.gov.

increased by 660 feet (200 m) between 1979 to 1999. Also, the stratosphere, from 9 miles to 14 miles (14.5 km to 22.5 km) up, is cooling—a result of the depletion of ozone, a greenhouse gas, in this atmospheric level.

These temperature trends are not limited to the United States or North America. Scientists have been reconstructing historical European temperatures by proxy methods back to 1500. They have found that the coldest winter on record was the winter of 1708–1709; the hottest summer took place in 2003. In the last half century, the average low temperature has risen about 1.8°F (1°C); there have been fewer extremely cold days and more frequent extremely hot days.[7]

A Heat Wave in Europe

Europeans enjoy a milder climate, one less prone to extremes, than that of North America. Winters in northern Europe are generally warmer and damper than in the northern United States; summers are cooler. The Gulf Stream current, which flows from

Houses in the village of Pailhares, France, burn as a result of the devastating heat wave that overwhelmed Europe in August 2003. Fred Dufour/AFP/Getty Images.

the tropics off the coast of North America and into the North Atlantic Ocean, warms the atmosphere that arrives over Europe with the prevailing westerly winds, moderating the weather in cities at relatively high latitudes.

The summer of 2003, however, was an exception. A record-setting heat wave brought rising maximum temperatures in the daytime and minimum temperatures at night. Many homes in Europe do not have air conditioning systems, and without the usual night cooling effect, thousands of houses across Europe were turned into sweltering ovens.

Not accustomed to the physical effects of high temperatures, many people suffered heat exhaustion, heat stroke, and dehydration. In France, approximately fifteen thousand people lost their lives, the highest death toll of any country. There were seven thousand deaths in Germany, more than four thousand each in Spain and Italy, and more than two thousand in Britain, which recorded a 100°F (37.78°C) day for the first time since reliable temperature records have been kept.[8]

The total approximate death toll of thirty-five thousand represents the highest number of casualties of any single weather event in Europe, ever. In fact, estimates made by the Earth Policy Institute in 2006, after more time had passed and more data had been collected, put the death toll at more than fifty-two thousand. Many of these deaths might have been prevented if the relatively wealthy nations of Europe had been better prepared. Public communication about the effects of heat exhaustion was poor; and many public health agencies were closed for the August holiday season, with doctors and medics away from their offices.

The European heat wave was an event statistically expected only once in several thousand years of "normal" modern climate. But it was not an isolated event; according to research noted by author Mark Lynas in his book *Six Degrees*, "the frequency of extremely hot days [in Europe] has tripled over the last century, and the length of heat waves on the continent has doubled."[9]

A Warming Future

As a consequence of recent trends in global average temperature, most locations on the planet can expect more extremely hot days, more frequent heat waves, and less frequent cold spells. A longer season of frost-free days will extend the growing season in many places, and in some areas of North America this may result in a frost-free season longer by a full month or more. There are also negative consequences for agriculture, however. Heat and drought damage to crops will increase; hot spells may raise the costs of storage for certain crops; livestock herds may experience heat stress and death. Fruit trees may also be affected, as most varieties grown in temperate climates need frost days in order to set the flowering buds necessary for later development of fruit.

In the Arctic, extreme heat events will contribute to the melting and shrinking of the polar ice cap, a phenomenon that has accelerated since 2000. As the open-water area increases at the pole, the erosive action of waves on the remaining ice will increase; in addition, as dark water absorbs more solar radiation than reflective snow and ice cover, the shrinking ice fields will contribute to atmospheric warming.

Tropical regions will be affected as well. Rising sea-surface temperatures and increased CO_2 concentrations in the atmosphere have coincided with a series of six mass bleaching episodes that have caused extensive damage to coral reefs in the Pacific Ocean and the Caribbean Sea. NOAA estimates that coral reefs could disappear completely in 50 to 75 years.[10]

More frequent heat waves will also have consequences for public health. Heat stroke and heat-related death are projected to rise (whereas cold-related deaths are projected to decrease). The decrease in days of frost may also allow disease organisms to flourish over a larger range, and for a longer time over the course of the year, than at present—a result that can affect food crops, livestock, and human health.

Public agencies in the United States can prepare for heat waves by informing the public, early and often, of the dangers. A

The Hot Gets Hotter

Death Valley, California, has always held the record as the single hottest place in the United States. Its highest day on record was 134°F (56.66°C), recorded on July 10, 1913—the hottest outdoor temperature ever recorded in the Western Hemisphere. In 1917, the valley recorded 43 days in a row with high temperatures exceeding 120°F (48.89°C). Several Death Valley heat records have been overtaken in recent years. The hottest month took place in July 2002, at an average temperature of 106°F (41.11°C). On July 13 of that year, the temperature ranged from a low of 100°F (37.7°C) to a high of 127°F (52.77°C), giving an average of 113.5°F (45.27°C). And in 2001, Death Valley recorded 154 days in a row with a high temperature of 100°F (37.8°C) or more—a record exceeded only by a stretch of 161 days of 100-degree-plus temperatures recorded at Marble Bar, Australia.

new Heat Health Watch/Warning System has been in use since 2007 at more than twenty U.S. weather-forecasting stations. In France, the city of Paris keeps a registry of elderly persons, who are especially susceptible to heat stroke and who are to be contacted by phone, or by a visit, whenever the temperature rises above 88°F (31°C).

Individuals can also prepare for heat waves by installing awnings and heavy drapes to block direct sunlight, insulating their homes effectively, installing attic fans and air conditioning units, using weather stripping and storm windows to prevent the loss of cool air in the house, and having a plan to evacuate to cooler public buildings in case of a power failure. A close watch on weather forecasts during the summer will also help individuals prepare for the dangers of prolonged, scorching temperatures— the quietest but also deadliest effect of the earth's steadily rising temperature.

Notes

1. "Heat and Humidity," *Weather Explained.* www.weatherexplained.com.
2. Institute for the Study of Society and Environment, *Heat Wave Awareness Project, ISSE.* www.isse.ucar.edu.
3. United States Environmental Protection Agency, *Temperature Changes,* www.epa.gov.
4. Goddard Institute for Space Studies, *Global Temperature Trends: 2008 Annual Summation.* http://data.giss.nasa.gov.
5. Center for American Progress Action Fund, "NCDC: Second Hottest June on Record," *Climate Progress,* July 16, 2009. http://climateprogress.org.
6. Gerald Meehl, Claudia Tebaldi, and Doug Nychka, "Changes in Frost Days in Simulations of Twentyfirst [*sic*] Century Climate," *Climate Dynamics,* vol. 23, August 20, 2004, pp. 495–512.
7. Jürg Luterbacher, Daniel Dietrich, Elena Xoplaki, Martin Grosjean, and Heinz Wanner, "European Seasonal and Annual Temperature Variability, Trends, and Extremes Since 1500," *Science,* vol. 303, March 5, 2004, pp. 1499–1503.
8. Shaoni Bhattacharya, "European Heatwave Caused 35,000 Deaths," *NewScientist,* October 10, 2003. www.newscientist.com.
9. Mark Lynas, *Six Degrees: Our Future on a Hotter Planet.* Washington, DC: National Geographic, 2008, p. 81.
10. European Project on Ocean Acidification, "Coral Reefs Being Destroyed by Global Warming, Acidification," *Ocean Acidification,* December 18, 2007. http://oceanacidification.wordpress.com.

CHAPTER 3

Drought

A drought is an extended period of unusually low precipitation. Behind this simple concept is the most damaging of all weather extremes. In the past, entire civilizations have been destroyed by extended periods of drought. Drought affects more of the planet, and with more widespread and deadly effects, than tropical storms, heat waves, or flooding caused by heavy rainfall or snowmelt.[1]

To measure drought, meteorologists employ several statistical tools, including the Palmer Drought Severity Index. Developed by Wayne Palmer in the 1960s, the Palmer Index is a formula that uses temperature and precipitation readings to measure the severity of extended periods of minimal rainfall. Where zero indicates a normal year, negative numbers on the Palmer Index increase as a drought worsens. A negative four or lower indicates a severe drought—the reading for large areas of the Rocky Mountains, southern California, and the southeastern United States in 2009. Positive numbers indicate rainfall that is higher than normal, which is the case for some areas of the Northeast and the northern Great Plains.

The effect of global warming on drought conditions is complex and uncertain, because drought is a local phenomenon that is affected by several factors apart from climate. Research into temperature and precipitation shows a general increase in both rainfall and temperature over the continental United States during the past fifty years. Climate models predict an intensification of drought conditions if the temperature trend continues, especially in the western and southwestern United States, regions that have been continuously under drought conditions over several decades.[2]

The Dust Bowl

The Dust Bowl of the 1930s was the worst drought in the history of the United States. The entire Great Plains region was affected, from the Rio Grande River to the prairies of Minnesota and Montana; the drought also reached into the Canadian "prairie provinces" of Manitoba, Saskatchewan, and Alberta. Rainfall amounts fell almost to zero in some years, drying out topsoil and destroying crops. The naturally occurring high winds in the region blew enormous clouds of soil, dust, and debris across hundreds of miles of open land; on especially bad days, black dust clouds dimmed skies throughout the eastern United States. Millions of discouraged farmers migrated from the Midwest to California and other points on the West Coast. This migration depopulated such states as Oklahoma and Kansas and contributed to the many economic woes of the Great Depression.

Several unusual but natural climate events caused the Dust Bowl drought. In the tropical Pacific Ocean, sea-surface temperatures were cooler than normal, while the tropical Atlantic was warmer than usual. As a result of this change in temperatures, the jet stream changed its course. This mass of upper-level air blows eastward across North America, bringing precipitation (in a normal year) to the Great Plains. With the jet stream moving to the south, however, rainfall in the Midwest lessened. Less moisture in the soil reduced surface evaporation; a loss of cloud cover increased the rate of evaporation. With less water vapor from the ground feeding the natural summer rainfall, a negative feedback loop occurred—in which conditions reinforced each other—and the drought conditions worsened.

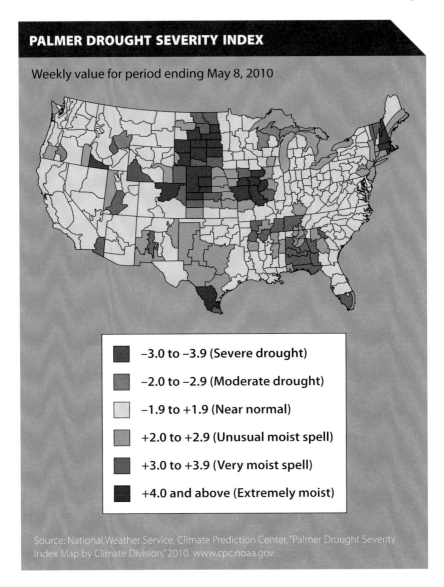

PALMER DROUGHT SEVERITY INDEX

Weekly value for period ending May 8, 2010

- ■ –3.0 to –3.9 (Severe drought)
- ■ –2.0 to –2.9 (Moderate drought)
- □ –1.9 to +1.9 (Near normal)
- ■ +2.0 to +2.9 (Unusual moist spell)
- ■ +3.0 to +3.9 (Very moist spell)
- ■ +4.0 and above (Extremely moist)

Source: National Weather Service, Climate Prediction Center, "Palmer Drought Severity Index Map by Climate Division," 2010. www.cpc.noaa.gov.

Drought in the Sahel

Another sea-surface temperature shift has caused a drought that has lasted for decades in the Sahel region of Africa. Lying between the Sahara Desert and the rain forest region of central Africa, the Sahel has been prone to drought throughout its history.

Africa's Sahel region has suffered drought for decades, which has driven much of its former population into cities. Melanie Stetson Freeman/The Christian Science Monitor/Getty Images.

A natural cycle known as the Atlantic Multidecadal Oscillation (AMO) is mainly responsible for these regular droughts. The AMO shifts sea-surface temperatures over the mid-Atlantic from warmer to colder and back again over a period of about seventy years. Cold years reduce the rainfall over the Sahel region; warm years increase precipitation. Currently the AMO is in a warming phase that is scheduled to peak about 2020.

Nevertheless, even in a normal year, less than 4 inches (100 mm) of rain falls in most parts of the Sahel. The rain occurs over a period of just a few weeks, leaving crops vulnerable to long dry spells that last for months and often longer. Periodically, the AMO and other factors shift the monsoon rains that sweep across this region from the Atlantic Ocean to the south, leaving the Sahel dry for years at a time.

These Sahelian droughts have been part of Earth's climate record for more than a millennium. In the seventh century, Arab caravans traveling through the Sahel from the Middle East recorded unusually dry conditions. Another drought began in the fourteenth century, lasting about two hundred years while the northern hemisphere was going through the Little Ice Age, a period that also brought colder sea-surface temperatures and drought conditions to South America and Asia. In the early twentieth century, rainfall increased in the Sahel until reaching a peak in 1936, which also happened to be the worst year of the Dust Bowl drought in North America.

Since the 1950s, the Sahel has suffered one of the worst droughts in recorded history—a 50-year period of scarce rainfall, desertification, and famine. The drought region extends across the continent, from Senegal in the west to Sudan in the east, where scarce resources and failed harvests have caused further suffering in a time of civil war. Areas of Mali and Niger once populated by Tuareg nomads and Fula herders have become arid deserts inhabited by a scattered, struggling population. If conditions persist, there will be further environmental damage and continued migration of people out of rural areas of Africa and into the cities.

The current drought in the Sahel is a natural cyclical phenomenon worsened by social and economic conditions. Overcultivation of the land, as well as overgrazing by livestock, has destroyed the topsoil layer essential for crops. In the countryside, herders and planters have few alternative economic activities.

The future outlook does not improve with scientific models based on rising greenhouse gas levels and anthropogenic climate change. According to a study of the Intergovernmental Panel on Climate Change (IPCC), these conditions will reinforce the cyclical changes in sea-surface temperatures, intensifying the AMO temperature range and worsening drought conditions in the Sahel during the twenty-first century.[3]

The result in the Sahel will be continued migration away from affected areas, and conflict over resources among people who remain. Farmers will abandon their struggling acreages, while livestock herders who lose their cattle will be hard-pressed to rebuild herds in times of drought and shortage. The migration of drought refugees into the cities of central and West Africa places even more stress on urban centers and threatens further social disruption to the struggling nations of the Sahel region.

Australia's Big Dry

In the early years of the twenty-first century, a severe drought struck Australia, a massive island continent that includes some of the most arid territory on the planet. Rainfall in the Murray-Darling river basin, the agricultural breadbasket of southeastern Australia, fell drastically, reducing water reservoirs and nearly drying up the entire watershed. With a rise in temperatures, the rate of surface evaporation increased. The drought was so severe that scientists have placed its chances of occurring as once in every thousand years. Mike Rann, the leader of the South Australian state government, commented that "What we're seeing with this drought is a frightening glimpse of the future with global warming."[4]

By 2008, more than half of all the cultivated and pasture land in Australia was struggling with drought conditions. The growing of cotton, which requires a steady and copious supply of water, came to a standstill. Dairy and sheep farmers lost entire herds. The reservoirs serving Sydney, the nation's largest city, fell to less than half of their capacity. In the fall of that year, the Murray-Darling system, which provides about 75 percent of all the drinking water in Australia and 85 percent of the water used to irrigate Australian crops, was flowing at its lowest level in recorded history.

For years, Australian politicians had expressed skepticism about anthropogenic climate change. Along with the United States, Australia refused to join the Kyoto Protocol, an agreement that came into effect in 2005, in which more than a hundred nations pledged to reduce their emissions of greenhouse gases. Australia protested the negative economic impact of forcing a reduction in emissions by its mining and energy industries.

Critics of this policy pointed out that Australia had the highest per-capita greenhouse gas emissions in the world. Prime Minister John Howard answered that the Kyoto Protocol would prove to be a flawed and ineffective agreement, as it excused developing nations such as India and China from the required emissions reductions.

Although he may have had some standing in his assessment of Kyoto, by 2009 Howard was changing his skeptical stance on global, human-induced climate change. Facing an election campaign while the Australian public demanded solutions for the drought, Howard announced his acceptance of the scientific case for anthropogenic global warming. He publicly supported "green energy" projects, and his government allocated payments to businesses and farmers directly affected by the drought. Howard also promoted the development of nuclear power to replace coal-fired energy plants, which are heavy emitters of carbon dioxide and other greenhouse gases.

Scientists in Australia predicted continuing drought conditions and rising temperatures through the twenty-first century. The IPCC report of 2007 pointed out the chance of increased brush fires, more frequent cyclone activity, and damage to the Great Barrier Reef in the waters off the coast of eastern Australia. According to several climate models, there is a chance that if the drought eventually breaks, and global temperatures continue to rise, the country will continue to suffer lower-than-normal precipitation levels. One study observed that: "The future mean annual rainfall projections from the 23 GCMs [general circulation models] per degree global warming range from −9 to +4 percent averaged across southeast Australia, −16 to 0 percent averaged across southwest Western Australia and −7 to +6 percent averaged across northern Australia."[5]

As a relatively wealthy, developed nation, Australia can take measures to adapt and adjust to its current drought. Severe water-use restrictions are in place in Sydney and other cities. Farmers are encouraged to use recycled "gray water" for irrigation purposes, and the government is offering rebates to buyers of water tanks and reservoirs. New desalination plants will process seawater into a usable form of freshwater. The election of Prime Minister Kevin Rudd also changed Australia's stance on the Kyoto Protocol, which the Australian government signed in December 2007.

The California Crisis

In any one location, several different factors may contribute to a drought. A higher average temperature increases the rate of evaporation from the soil and from water reservoirs. In drought-stricken areas, higher precipitation in mountainous areas does not offset higher evaporation in the low-lying watersheds they supply with drinking and irrigation water. Regular oscillations in sea-surface temperatures, such as the El Niño warming that occurs in the eastern Pacific Ocean every decade or so, can also affect climate over large areas, bringing drastic changes in precipitation patterns. Human actions and government policy can also play a part.

"If the mechanisms we think work hold true, then we'll get big droughts in the West again."

Combined, all of these conditions have brought a severe, years-long drought to the western United States. In the San Joaquin Valley of central California, the drought has affected farms and commercial orchards that supply a large percentage of the nation's fruits, edible nuts, and vegetables. The shortage of water has been amplified by federal restrictions on water use.

In an effort to protect an endangered small fish, the delta smelt, the U.S. Fish and Wildlife Service restricts the pumping of water from the Sacramento-San Joaquin Delta via aqueducts to Central Valley farms and to communities farther south that rely on the aqueducts for drinking water. The result has been an economic malaise and rising unemployment among the farming communities of this region.

To combat the drought, Los Angeles and other western cities have adopted strict limits on water use. Residents can use their lawn sprinklers for just fifteen minutes a day, on Mondays and Thursdays only, and never between the hours of 9 A.M. and 4 P.M. If they successfully reduce their use of water, they are granted a reduction in their water bills, which arrive every two months. If they use more than their allotment, they are penalized. Teams of "drought busters" roam the city's neighborhoods, verifying that residents are obeying the water use restrictions.

The restrictions have lessened demand for water, alleviating the shortages brought about by the drought. But the drought is causing more problems in California than a shortage of drinking and sprinkling water. Dry regions in the state are more prone to brush fires, which occur naturally in this region but also pose a dangerous threat to homes that were built in undeveloped areas without adequate regard to fire hazard. The prospect of a continuing rise in global average temperatures does not improve the outlook. "The medieval warm period a thousand years ago was a very small forcing compared to what is going on with global warming now," comments meteorologist Mark Cane in *With Speed and Violence*. "But it was still strong enough to cause a 300- to 400-year drought in the western U.S. That could be an analogue for what will happen under anthropogenic warming. If the mechanisms we think work hold true, then we'll get big droughts in the West again."[6]

Drought: Future Impacts

There are direct and indirect impacts brought by an extended drought. The direct impacts include a reduced area of land for the cultivation of crops and for the support of livestock; losses in the forestry and fishing industries; a higher risk of wildfires, which destroy productive land and contribute to ever-higher levels of carbon dioxide in the atmosphere; a loss of water available for

Drought: The Civilization Killer

In the early Middle Ages, when the Medieval Warm Period was allowing Vikings to settle Iceland and later the western coast of Greenland, the Mayan civilization of Mexico and Central America was dying out. Entire cities were abandoned, and elaborate temples and palaces fell into disuse. The Mayan people scattered into small, isolated farming communities. The central government collapsed, and the Maya found themselves unable to resist conquest by Spanish explorers and colonizers beginning in the sixteenth century.

Historians believe that a long-term drought, a component of the climate variance known as the Medieval Warm Period, played an important role in the collapse of the Maya and of the Anasazi civilization, which collapsed in the American Southwest around the same time. Scientists have concluded that a relatively minor fluctuation in solar radiation was to blame for these climate variances, and that the same kind of variation in the sea-surface temperature of the Pacific is contributing to the drought now affecting California and the southwestern states. Global warming will not help the situation: At the current pace, according to Wallace S. Broecker and Robert Kunzig in their book *Fixing Climate*, human beings are contributing to a variance in solar radiation five times the intensity reached during the Medieval Warm Period:

> Maybe the current warming, instead of bringing a mega-drought to the West, will be strong enough to overwhelm the feedback mechanism that turns warming into cooling in the eastern Pacific; the result might then be a more [El] Niño-like future and more rain for the West rather than less. Maybe the American West will get lucky, in other words, and the worst effects of global warming will be felt elsewhere. But at the moment it does not seem likely.

household use and irrigation; and permanent damage to wildlife habitat. Droughts also can worsen plant diseases and insect infestations, and can contribute to soil erosion.

Indirect, long-range impacts include rising prices for farmers and, ultimately, consumers; foreclosures on unprofitable farms and their property; and a continuing strain on public resources to develop new sources of water and alleviate the economic impacts. An economic depression in the farming sector ripples through the entire economy, affecting banking and insurance companies, as well as manufacturing industries that supply the agricultural market. Rising unemployment and a loss of tax revenue are further indirect effects.

Sustained drought conditions may prove to be the most severe consequences of climate change. The Colorado River, which supplies much of the southwestern United States with water, has fallen to an average flow of 3 million acre-feet a year—less than a quarter of its twentieth-century annual average of 13 million acre-feet.[7] Major cities, such as Sydney and Los Angeles, have already declared water emergencies, restricting the use of water by their millions of residents. Falling levels in hydropower reservoirs may lead to shortages of electricity in areas that depend on this source of energy.

Drought may also reduce the production of food in agricultural centers such as the U.S. Midwest and the Murray-Darling basin of Australia. This will lead to rising prices, a lower standard of living for many people, conflict over remaining water resources, and in some areas famine conditions. Migration from drought-affected areas, as in western Africa, will also cause social and political disruption in the affected nations. "Climate refugees" are already posing serious problems in nations of the Sahel region of Africa. Most of these refugees do not return to their homes even after a drought abates, placing a permanent stress on the infrastructure of crowded cities where they have settled.

Drought will also force drastic changes in the natural environment. The natural range of flora and fauna will shift away from drought-affected areas and contribute to the expansion of deserts. A loss in wetlands can eliminate or drastically reduce local populations of birds, fish, mammals, and plants. An increased rate of forest fires also degrades air and water resources.

The options for dealing with long-term drought are difficult and expensive, and the immediate benefits not always apparent. These include better water management, in which dry areas make use of reservoirs and crop terraces in order to control the use of water. Lines of trees known as windbreaks, planted to lessen the destruction of topsoil by cyclonic winds, have also been used in the United States and the Sahel region. But these measures require investment, and drought remains an especially tough problem for societies in which rural farmers have less political clout and economic influence than urban populations, which have their own pressing needs and agendas.

Notes

1. National Drought Mitigation Center, "Impacts of Drought." http://drought.unl.edu.
2. David R. Easterling et al., "The Effects of Temperature and Precipitation Trends on U.S. Drought," *Geophysical Research Letters*, vol. 34, 2007.
3. David B. Enfield and Luis Cid-Serrano, "Secular and Multidecadal Warmings in the North Atlantic and Their Relationships with Major Hurricane Activity," *International Journal of Climatology*, vol. 30, 2010, pp. 174–184. www.aoml.noaa.gov.
4. Reuters News Service, "Australia Drought Could Be Worst in 1,000 Years," *MSNBC*, November 9, 2006. www.msnbc.msn.com.
5. F.H.S. Chiew et al., "Assessment of rainfall simulations from global climate models and implications for climate change impact on runoff studies," Modelling and Simulation Society of Australia and New Zealand. www.mssanz.org.au.
6. Fred Pearce, *With Speed and Violence: Why Scientists Fear Tipping Points in Climate Change*. Boston: Beacon Press, 2007, p. 173.
7. "U.S. Drought News," *WaterWebster*. www.waterwebster.com.

CHAPTER 4

Rainfall and Flooding

The effect of global warming on rainfall around the globe is an extremely complex calculation that is still under debate by scientists. Heavy precipitation is a local event that is dependent on several varying factors. Scattered weather stations cannot measure rainfall uniformly over a large area, and they can easily miss the occurrence of an unusually heavy rainstorm in any one place.

Precipitation extremes are gauged by frequency (how often they occur), by measured intensity (how much precipitation they bring), and by return (the amount of time between occurrences). Measured extremes differ by location: An extreme event in the arid southwestern deserts, for example, has a much lower threshold of frequency and intensity than one that takes place over the rainy northwest coast. For each region of the country, extreme rainfall carries a different meaning.

Behind the complex measurements and models lies the question of global warming's effect on a basic mechanism of weather: the hydrologic cycle. This is a natural phenomenon that is essential to all life on Earth. Evaporation of water from the sea builds up water vapor in the atmosphere. Wind carries this water vapor over landmasses. When conditions are right, the water vapor condenses and falls to the earth in the form of rain, snow, or other forms of precipitation.

Warming of the earth's surface and the atmosphere by greenhouse gases has an effect on this natural cycle. When the sea-surface temperature rises, the difference in vapor pressure between the sea and the atmosphere increases. This brings about a faster rate of evaporation, which raises the concentration of water vapor in the atmosphere. At the same time, a warmer atmosphere can hold more water vapor. Under these conditions, the hydrologic cycle intensifies. The increased rate depends on the amount of the temperature rise. Water vapor, like carbon dioxide and other compounds, is a heat-trapping greenhouse gas, one that is even more effective than carbon dioxide at trapping solar radiation. An increasing rate of evaporation brings about an expanding cloud cover; the rising and expanding rain clouds that form over larger areas of Earth's surface also trap solar radiation, increasing the rate of warming.

There is evidence that the earth's hydrologic cycle has already been affected by the recent warming of the atmosphere. Satellites have detected a rise in the concentration of water vapor of 1.3 percent per decade since 1988.[1] Another clue is the fact that nighttime minimum temperatures are rising twice as fast as maximum readings during the day. Increasing cloudiness and humidity at night, and faster daytime evaporation (which cools the atmosphere), would have this effect—and both are consequences of a faster hydrologic cycle.

Instead of more frequent rainfall, the increasing rate of precipitation is coming as heavier rainfall. The changes in the rate of precipitation are not uniform around the globe. In some regions, including Africa and Australia, local weather conditions have become much drier. In the tropical latitudes of the Pacific Ocean, where sea-surface temperatures and evaporation rates are rising, rainfall has increased. In the United States, a higher percentage of total precipitation is coming during extreme events (defined, by one measure, as more than two inches of rainfall in a twenty-four-hour period).

Around the globe, precipitation has increased by up to 10 percent due to the faster hydrologic cycle.[2] Rainfall is increasing faster in higher latitudes, and the fastest near the north and south poles, where atmospheric warming has been significant and where the shrinking of ice fields exposes more open water—in turn leading to faster evaporation and more fuel for the hydrologic engine.

Effects of a Faster Hydrologic Cycle

In some areas, an enhanced hydrologic cycle, fewer days of frost and freezing temperatures, and higher rates of precipitation may prove beneficial to agriculture. An increased amount of carbon dioxide in the atmosphere also helps crops. As a result of this fertilization effect, growing seasons will lengthen, the area of cultivable land will increase, and in some areas a wider variety of crops will be grown.

At the same time, however, these conditions threaten serious damage, both from the heavier rainfall and from the change in temperatures and length of seasons. Shorter winter seasons reduce the melting of ice and snow in the spring. Each year, this snowmelt allows dry underground reservoirs to recharge. Groundwater that feeds rivers and streams lessens, reducing the amount of water available in dry seasons for the irrigation of crops and the supply of drinking water.

In places that experience more intense storms and heavier precipitation, flooding threatens more damage, forcing farms and communities to undertake new flood-control measures such as dams and levees. Topsoil erosion will worsen, as will the environmental damage caused by the runoff of soil polluted by fertilizers and pesticides. All of these effects imply a higher cost for the production of basic foodstuffs and livestock feed, raising prices for consumers.

In the United States, scientists have measured higher surface temperatures throughout the country as well as a higher concentration of water vapor in the upper atmosphere. Average annual precipitation in the United States has increased by 7 percent over the twentieth century; heavy precipitation events (defined as the heaviest 5 percent of all storms) have increased by 14 percent,

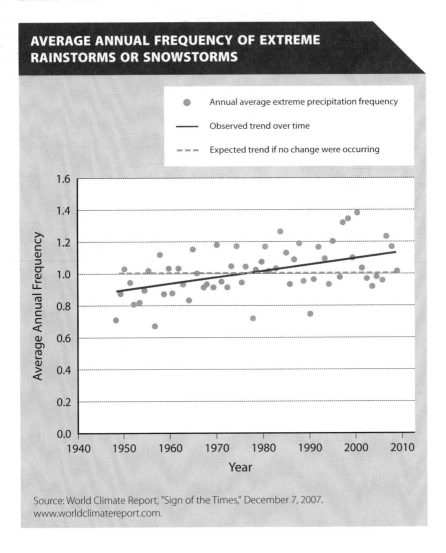

AVERAGE ANNUAL FREQUENCY OF EXTREME RAINSTORMS OR SNOWSTORMS

● Annual average extreme precipitation frequency

— Observed trend over time

- - - Expected trend if no change were occurring

Average Annual Frequency

Year

Source: World Climate Report, "Sign of the Times," December 7, 2007. www.worldclimatereport.com.

and very heavy events (the top 1 percent) have increased by 20 percent.[3]

Extreme storms bringing heavy rainfall or snowfall are becoming more frequent. The trend has been measured since the early 1930s and the frequency has been increasing at a faster rate in the last few decades. Since 1948, according to one study, extreme storms have become about 24 percent more frequent throughout the country. Heavy storms have also become more frequent over the Great Lakes region and the upper Midwest.[4]

"In addition to triggering more rainfall, global warming could also increase the occurrence of drought."

By some accounts, however, intensified drought conditions in drought-prone areas may also result from increasing temperatures and a faster hydrologic cycle. "You might expect droughts to diminish on a global basis as rainfall goes up," comments Robert Henson in *The Rough Guide to Climate Change*. "But higher temperatures not only allow more rain-producing moisture to enter the atmosphere—they also suck more water out of the parched terrain where it hasn't been raining. Thus, in addition to triggering more rainfall, global warming could also increase the occurrence of drought."[5]

Clouds and Warming

The natural formation of clouds comes about as a result of water vapor condensation in air, which is cooler above the ground than at the surface. Clouds have various, sometimes conflicting effects on warming of the surface and the amount of precipitation. Where clouds occur, they reflect from 10 to 90 percent of the sunlight that reaches the earth (depending on their height, type, and thickness). At higher reflectivity, this has the effect of cooling the ground or sea at the surface.

Clouds have a warming effect as well. Solar radiation that manages to reach the ground and then is reflected is absorbed, to some extent, by water vapor in the atmosphere, which is present in higher concentrations in clouded areas. This keeps the ground warmer, and more humid, than it would be without cloud cover.

The effects cancel out each other to some extent, and by some measures clouds actually cool the planet. One study found that

Mumbai's July 26, 2005, Rain Event

The monsoon is critical for agriculture and industry in South and Southeast Asia. Global climate models suggest that a general warming will bring heavier rainfall and a warmer and wetter monsoon season in India. It will also increase the risk of severe rainfall and flooding events.

One harbinger of what may be to come occurred on July 26, 2005, when the rains poured down on Mumbai, India. More than one meter of rain fell on the teeming city in the span of twenty-four hours. Neighborhoods near sea level were flooded with three feet of water. Offices, schools, and the airport were closed. The Mumbai Stock Exchange shut down. Animal carcasses floated by the thousands through the city streets. The sewage system overflowed to contaminate houses, parks, streets, and sidewalks. Dysentery and cholera, deadly waterborne diseases, spread rapidly.

The events of July 26 in Mumbai illustrate the results of intensifying precipitation in crowded cities, yet the most devastating effect of a changing monsoon pattern arrives in the countryside. If monsoons change their timing and intensity, farmers can no longer plant with any certainty of collecting a harvest. Water supplies can be disrupted, and food shortages result. In countries where many people depend on farming to feed themselves and their families, this shift could have devastating long-term economic, social, and political effects.

clouds reflect 45 watts of sunlight per square meter back into space, while sunlight that passes through them is reflected at the rate of 30 watts to a square meter of ground.[6]

In an era of global warming, decreasing cloud cover is one possible result that could contribute to rising temperatures at the surface. Because the net effect of cloudiness is a reflection of 15 watts of sunlight per square meter, a reduction of daytime cloud cover would increase the amount of solar radiation received at the surface. Another feedback mechanism is thus created, with retreating cloud cover contributing to rising average temperatures, which further reduce cloudiness.

Urban Pollution and the Heat Island

The anthropogenic effect of urban pollution from car and factory exhaust may also be contributing to increasing precipitation as well. Particles in the atmosphere, car exhaust, dust, and other pollutants provide a nucleus of matter around which water vapor more easily condenses. As a result, days of heavier atmospheric pollution also tend to be days of more frequent and heavier precipitation. One study compared rainfall amounts over the southeastern United States on the seven days of the week, and found precipitation generally more intense on weekdays—when commuter traffic is heaviest—than on weekends.[7]

This anthropogenic effect on climate parallels the heat island effect, in which urbanized areas tend to be warmer than the surrounding countryside. The heat island is a result of the construction of buildings, roads, parking lots, and other artificial surfaces that prevent the natural absorption of radiation by the ground and tend to reflect that radiation back into the atmosphere. Scientists studying temperature trends must adjust their readings to account for the heat island effect, and some of those studying precipitation are also taking into account the contribution of urban pollution levels as well.

If skeptics of the global warming hypothesis lack an example of human effects on climate, they can examine the urban pollution/precipitation link as well as the heat island, a very localized case of anthropogenic warming. Perception of heavy storms, flooding, and other extreme weather, however, may be changing as well. Increased media coverage, newspaper and magazine accounts, the ongoing climate change controversy, and The Weather Channel all are having an effect on public perception of the climate and how it may be changing. One study by Robert

Balling and Randall Cerveny at Arizona State University found that the public is three times as likely to see a media story on severe weather than thirty years ago, and that "Damage from severe weather has increased over this period, but this upward trend disappears when inflation, population growth, population redistribution and wealth are taken into account."[8]

The Consequences of Extreme Precipitation

Extreme precipitation can be more damaging than ordinary rain or snow events. Heavy rainfalls can cause flooding over a wide area, as swollen streams and rivers overtop levees and embankments far downstream. Also, Paul Douglas notes in *Restless Skies*, "much of what was once farmland is now suburban subdivisions and parking lots. Rainwater and melting snow can't soak into the paved-over ground, so they run off into streets, storm sewers and rivers faster than ever, increasing the risk of disaster."[9]

Standing water in city streets snarls traffic; flooded homes, offices, and stores require expensive repairs, cleaning, and disinfection. Flash floods that occur in dry streambeds can cause property damage and loss of life. Flooding can also carry away valuable topsoil, thus leaving affected areas less productive and driving up the price of basic foodstuffs.

Floodwaters carry pollutants, including chemical fertilizers and pesticides, and in some cases untreated sewage. These contaminants affect water quality in rivers and lakes, as well as reservoirs that provide a sorely needed supply of fresh drinking water to urban areas. Poor societies that lack water-treatment facilities, or the means to construct preventive flood barriers, will suffer this consequence the most.

Heavy rain and flooding (along with higher temperatures) also benefit the array of water-borne diseases that plague nations in the tropics. With a greater amount of the surface flooded or covered by standing water, malaria, a disease carried by mosquitoes, could spread beyond the tropical zones, where it is now

Increased rainfall could result in more disasters such as the flooding that occurred in Illinois, Wisconsin, Minnesota, and Ohio in August 2007, killing twenty-two people. Scott Olson/ Getty Images.

confined, to affect a greater range. Other diseases boosted in this way include Lyme disease, dengue fever, and encephalitis.

With rising temperatures, and higher nightly minimums, precipitation will fall more frequently as rain and less frequently as snow, thus increasing the risk of heavy runoff and flooding. Human societies have developed many different mechanisms to control rivers and deal with the threat of floods. But these artificial means of coping with natural destruction can themselves have unintended consequences.

Levees built along the Mississippi River, for example, now prevent the natural spring inundation of floodplains that border several hundred miles of the river's course. This thwarts the natural purpose of a floodplain: to absorb the spring snowmelt and allow the river to gradually siphon off several dozen feet of excess flow before it reaches the river's mouth. Channeling the Mississippi in this way allows more development along the river, but it also forces even worse flooding downstream as the river carries its full charge of spring water farther south than it would naturally.

Notes

1. Kevin E. Trenberth, John Fasullo, and Lesley Smith, "Trends and Variability in Column-Integrated Atmospheric Water Vapor," *Climate Dynamics*. www.cgd.ucar .edu.
2. Fred Pearce, *With Speed and Violence: Why Scientists Fear Tipping Points in Climate Change*. Boston: Beacon Press, 2007, p. 20.
3. B. Geerts and E. Linacre, "Is the Hydrologic Cycle Intensifying?" University of Wyoming, College of Engineering and Applied Science, Atmospheric Science, n.d. www. das.uwyo.edu.
4. Travis Madsen and Emily Figdor, "When It Rains, It Pours: Global Warming and the Rising Frequency of Extreme Precipitation in the United States," Environment Colorado Research and Policy Center, n.d. http://cdn.publicinterestnetwork.org.
5. Robert Henson, *The Rough Guide to Climate Change*. London and New York: Rough Guides, Ltd., 2006, p. 56.
6. Richard C.J. Somerville, *The Forgiving Air: Understanding Environmental Change*. Berkeley: University of California Press, 1998, p. 70.
7. "Rain Slows Down on Weekends in Southeast," *Bulletin of the American Meteorological Society*, April 2008, p. 431.
8. Robert C. Balling and Randall S. Cerveny, "Compilation and Discussion of Trends in Severe Storms in the United States: Popular Perception v. Climate Reality," *Natural Hazards*, vol. 29, June 2003, p. 103.
9. Paul Douglas, *Restless Skies: The Ultimate Weather Book*. New York: Sterling, 2007, p. 54.

CHAPTER 5

Hurricanes and Tropical Cyclones

In the late summer of 2005, the most destructive storm in the history of the United States began gathering strength in the mid-Atlantic Ocean. Meteorologists named the system Tropical Depression Twelve. A westerly wave that originated off the west coast of Africa, and the scattered winds of another tropical depression, strengthened the storm. On August 24, while it was churning southeast of the Bahamas, the storm earned the name Hurricane Katrina.

Katrina traveled due west, striking southern Florida and then the Florida Keys, an island chain that ends at Key West, the southernmost point in the continental United States. At this point, Katrina was still a minor, Category 1 hurricane. Gradually, over the Gulf of Mexico, the storm grew larger and stronger. The waters of the gulf were warmer than usual, even for the summer. Katrina rapidly drew up heat and water vapor; its winds strengthened to 175 miles (280 km) per hour, and its counterclockwise-turning clouds spread across an area of 500 square miles (1,295 sq. km). The storm reached the extremely damaging, dangerous level of Category 5.

By Saturday, August 28, Katrina was moving due north, heading straight for the coastal regions of Louisiana, Mississippi, Alabama, and the northern Florida panhandle. It was threatening the destruction of coastal wetlands, river estuaries, barrier islands, and the city of New Orleans, which lay below sea level between the Mississippi River and Lake Pontchartrain. Katrina also posed a danger to new coastal communities where residents were building homes, hotels, business districts, resorts, and roads directly in the path of the powerful hurricanes that regularly make landfall in this region.

Hurricane Katrina

The center of Hurricane Katrina made landfall fifty miles east of New Orleans. The storm crashed into southeastern Louisiana, then the Mississippi Gulf Coast, as a Category 3, with top winds of 125 miles (200 km) per hour. In coastal cities such as Venice, Louisiana, and the Mississippi towns of Pass Christian, Pascagoula, and Waveland, the damage was catastrophic. A storm surge over twenty feet in height drowned hundreds of people, flooded homes, and swept away cars and trees. In some towns, not a single building was left standing.

The Saffir-Simpson Scale

In the 1950s, Herbert Saffir and Robert Simpson created the Saffir-Simpson Damage Potential Scale. This measured the strength of hurricanes by their top wind speeds. The scale runs from Category 1 to 5, with 5 being the strongest, a catastrophic storm with winds over 155 miles per hour. According to the National Weather Service, the official description of a Category 5 predicts that:

> Complete roof failure on many residences and industrial buildings will occur. Some complete building failures with small buildings blown over or away are likely. All signs blown down. Complete destruction of mobile homes (built in any year). Severe and extensive window and door damage will occur. Nearly all windows in high rise buildings will be dislodged and become airborne. Severe injury or death is likely for persons struck by wind-blown debris. . . .

New Orleans survived the winds, but not the storm surge. The waters of Lake Pontchartrain flooded the levees built by the U.S. Army Corps of Engineers after Hurricane Betsy struck in 1965. Over eight feet of water poured into the city's low-lying neighborhoods. Thousands of residents were left homeless. The storm broke up roads and railroads leading out of town. The electricity grid and water systems failed. Looters ran amok in the chaos as civil order broke down.

A powerful hurricane such as Katrina rarely makes landfall. Most tropical depressions weaken as they move north over cooler water. Others strike land before they can strengthen into major storms. Climatologists have discovered that hurricanes occur in long cycles, and since 1995 an active hurricane cycle has been taking place in the Atlantic Ocean. Warmer sea-surface temperatures in the Atlantic and the Gulf of Mexico feed these systems, making them stronger than they would be over cooler water.

Besides causing a human and natural catastrophe, Katrina posed important questions to climatologists. Was the warmer sea-surface temperature a natural event, or was it caused by human activity? Were the warming waters creating stronger, more frequent hurricanes? And would damaging hurricanes become more common in the future?

Cyclone Nargis

The waters of the Bay of Bengal touch several populous nations of south Asia. In the spring, these seas begin to warm rapidly. The quick evaporation of seawater into the humid atmosphere gives rise to tropical storms, known in Asia as cyclones. These dangerous weather systems strengthen over warm waters and follow zones of low pressure until making landfall. The seacoasts of Bangladesh, Myanmar, and India are heavily populated, and most of the communities have made few storm preparations. As a result, the death and destruction caused by cyclones is many times worse than hurricane damage in North America.

Cyclone Nargis hit Myanmar in May 2008, killing tens of thousands of people and leaving billions of dollars in damage. AP Images.

One of Asia's deadliest cyclones began as Tropical Cyclone 01B in April 2008. The storm formed in the Indian Ocean and moved to the northwest, skirting a ridge of high pressure that blocked its passage to the coast. It began to rotate and strengthen; as with hurricanes, it was helped by a lack of wind shear—crosswinds at high altitudes that cause intense turbulence and tend to break up storm systems. On April 28, meteorologists renamed Cyclone 01B as Cyclone Nargis. The next day, its winds reached 100 miles (160 km) per hour. Two days later, it turned to the east. On May 2, it reached the coast of Myanmar, the nation formerly known as Burma.

The delta of the Irrawaddy River spreads along the southern coast of Myanmar, where the river branches into a complex network of streams and irrigation canals. More than a million people there live at or near sea level, with few protective structures to prevent flooding from storm surge. Cyclone Nargis came ashore with strong winds and a sudden, immense tide of water that destroyed hundreds of villages. Houses were washed away or collapsed in the flood. More than one hundred thousand people died, fifty thousand went missing, and several million were left homeless.[1] Nargis became the deadliest cyclone in Asia since 1970, when Cyclone Bhola caused half a million deaths in Bangladesh.

Monsoons and Cyclones

The monsoon has been a regular annual occurrence along the coasts of south Asia for several million years. In the fall, as the Indian subcontinent cools, winds sweep down from the Himalaya Mountains to the north, lowering temperatures while the atmosphere gains moisture from the warm Bay of Bengal. Heavy rain is common in India during this northeast monsoon.

In the summer, the land begins to warm, the warming air rises, and zones of low pressure develop over India. The prevailing wind direction reverses, now blowing from the southwest. Clouds that form over the subcontinent move toward the Himalayas. As they rise with the elevation, the air cools, moisture condenses, and precipitation results.

A single monsoon season can bring several feet of rain to areas of India, Bangladesh, and other nations of the region. Farmers depend on the rains to irrigate their crops, while villages and towns need the monsoon to replenish their freshwater wells. But there is small difference between a normal monsoon and a damaging flood. When the rains remain heavy for several weeks, they can overwhelm structures such as dikes and canals. Crops are destroyed, homes are flooded, and wells are poisoned with storm runoff.

Cyclones frequently result during the transition between one monsoon and the next. While rapid evaporation from the warm sea surface continues, the rate of wind shear at high altitudes decreases. Wind shear, which results from wind moving at a different speed and direction at different levels in the atmosphere, disrupts cyclonic storm systems. When wind shear weakens, storms have more opportunity to develop.

Many climate models predict that warming sea-surface temperatures will bring about more frequent and stronger tropical storms. This is true in the Bay of Bengal as well as the mid-Atlantic Ocean. The warming atmosphere also tends to strengthen high-altitude wind shear, however. The contending influence of these two factors—wind shear and warming seas—will affect the future occurrence of cyclones and hurricanes.

Hurricane Formation

Hurricanes and cyclones originate as tropical depressions. A drop in barometric pressure, or the weight of the atmosphere over a single point, brings clouds, rain, and high winds. Climate systems gain strength over warm water. In the mid-Atlantic Ocean, prevailing winds in the late summer push tropical storms toward the west.

The planet's rotation causes the expanding storm to begin turning, a phenomenon known as the Coriolis effect, named for Gaspard-Gustave de Coriolis, a French scientist who studied it in the early nineteenth century. The Coriolis effect spins the storm counterclockwise in the northern hemisphere, clockwise in the southern hemisphere. As the wind strengthens, water evaporates rapidly from the surface of the sea. The warmer the water, the faster the evaporation, and the more powerful the storm.

Air moves toward the region of low barometric pressure. This gives rise to the hurricane's powerful winds. At the center of the storm, the pressure continues to fall as the storm forms a central column of rapidly rising warm air. Centrifugal force pushes the warm air and clouds outward, to the edges of the system. As it grows, the hurricane gradually develops a central low-pressure zone or "eye." In the strongest hurricanes, the eye is a cloudless region as much as 50 miles (80 km) across.

Hurricanes follow the path of least resistance into areas of lower barometric pressure. High pressure deflects the storms. Winds in the upper atmosphere also have an effect. Using pressure readings, wind speed and direction, and other factors, meteorologists can accurately predict the general direction of hurricanes—and more importantly, where they will make landfall.

A COMPARATIVE LOOK AT HURRICANE KATRINA

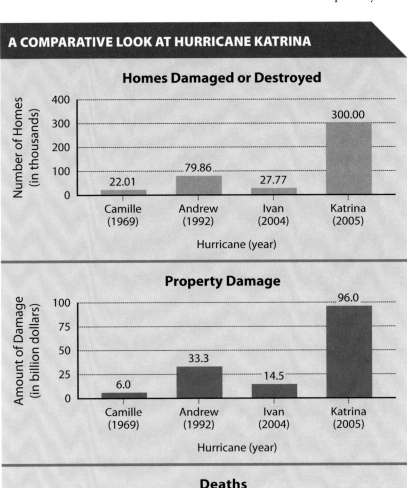

Homes Damaged or Destroyed

Number of Homes (in thousands)

- Camille (1969): 22.01
- Andrew (1992): 79.86
- Ivan (2004): 27.77
- Katrina (2005): 300.00

Hurricane (year)

Property Damage

Amount of Damage (in billion dollars)

- Camille (1969): 6.0
- Andrew (1992): 33.3
- Ivan (2004): 14.5
- Katrina (2005): 96.0

Hurricane (year)

Deaths

Number of Deaths

- Camille (1969): 335
- Andrew (1992): 61
- Ivan (2004): 57
- Katrina (2005): 1,330

Hurricane (year)

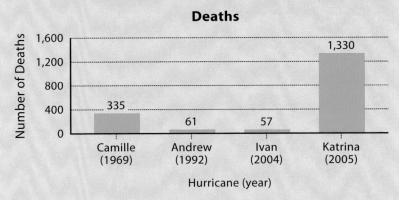

Source: *The Federal Response to Hurricane Katrina: Lessons Learned* (official White House report), February 2006, p. 7. http://georgewbush-whitehouse.archives.gov.

Although Hurricane Katrina devastated New Orleans in 2005, the storm also did substantial damage elsewhere along the U.S. Gulf Coast—including Biloxi, Mississippi, as shown here. Marianne Todd/Getty Images.

Well before Katrina, hurricanes caused massive damage and loss of life. A hurricane struck the coastal town of Galveston, Texas, in 1900 and killed about ten thousand people, even though the city was protected by a seventeen-foot seawall. The Labor Day Hurricane in the Florida Keys in 1935 wiped out entire towns, killed several thousand people, and destroyed an elevated railway linking the islands. Hurricane Betsy killed dozens of people in New Orleans in 1965. This fateful storm prompted the building of the city's levees, which, forty years later, failed in their mission: to withstand a Category 3 hurricane.

The AMO and Other Natural Factors

Scientists have discovered a natural cycle known as the Atlantic Multidecadal Oscillation, or AMO. This cycle has been repeating for thousands of years, since the last ice age ended (about ten thousand years ago). The AMO brought warmer waters to the Atlantic between 1926 and 1969. Ocean temperatures dropped

Witness to a Hurricane

Before scientists knew anything about hurricanes, travelers and explorers grew familiar with their terrible power. In his *History of the New World*, written in 1565, Girolamo Benzoni described one such storm that struck the Caribbean during a voyage of the explorer Christopher Columbus:

> At sunrise such a horrible, strong wind began that the inhabitants of the island thought they had never seen or heard anything like it before. The raging storm wind . . . came with great violence, as if it wanted to split heaven and earth apart from one another, and hurl everything to the ground . . . Meanwhile the wind blew with such great and terrible force that it ripped many large trees out of the earth by the roots and threw them over . . . The strong and frightful wind threw some entire houses and capitals including the people from the capital, tore them apart in the air and threw them down to the ground in pieces.

to cooler levels from 1970 to 1995. In these same years, few major hurricanes occurred. The same phenomenon began raising the temperature of the Atlantic Ocean in the mid-1990s. About this time, the number of hurricanes and their intensity began to increase.

There were other factors at work. The warm El Niño ocean current, which occurs every few years in the Pacific Ocean, affects the intensity of hurricanes in the Atlantic. The Bermuda High, a region of high atmospheric pressure, wanders from south to north and back again in the North Atlantic, steering hurricanes sometimes to the north, sometimes to the west.

Another factor was thermohaline circulation. In the deep ocean, density and temperature are key factors in the movement of great masses of water around the globe. Warmer water has a lower density, and it rises; colder water is denser, and it sinks. Salinity—the level of salt and other minerals dissolved in oceanic waters—also has an impact, with more salinity lending greater density.

The entire system of circulation originates at the poles, where cold winds and the melting of glaciers lower water temperature. The wind evaporates water at the surface, causing higher salinity and contributing to the cooling effect. The cold, heavy water drops and moves south toward the middle of the Atlantic Ocean.

Thermohaline circulation affects sea-surface temperatures and climate around the globe. As warm water rises and cold water falls, strong currents result. When conditions are right—a particularly strong, warm current appearing in the tropical latitudes near the equator—a busy hurricane season begins.

The Effect of Global Warming

The hurricane seasons that brought Katrina and other Category 5 storms in 2004 and 2005 may have been enhanced by the AMO, but a 2006 study by Kevin Trenberth of the U.S. National Center for Atmospheric Research found that the AMO had less than half the impact of anthropogenic global warming in bringing about the higher North Atlantic sea-surface temperatures in 2005.[2]

sea-surface tempuratures have been measured for a longer time, and more accurately, than hurricane strength and duration. Scientists can measure historical sea-surface tempuratures through the analysis of organisms such as shells and corals. The data show that over the past five decades, the global average sea-surface temperature has risen about 1°F, or about .55°C—a trend that correlates with the rise in the concentration of atmospheric carbon dioxide. Since 1988, scientists have also measured a 4 percent rise in the level of water vapor—basic hurricane fuel—over the ocean surface.[3]

Scientists have reached consensus on the fact that rising sea-surface temperatures bring about more frequent and stronger hurricanes. But the record of hurricane measurement is very short. Storm-tracking aircraft have been regularly measuring hurricane wind speeds only since the 1950s, a very brief span in Earth's climate history. Although meteorologists believed strongly in the link between rising sea-surface temperatures and increased hurricane strength, they had no statistic to measure the hurricane strength, other than wind speed, until meteorology professor Kerry Emanuel created the Power Dissipation Index (PDI) in 2005. The PDI is calculated by taking the maximum one-minute sustained winds of a storm every six hours, as long as the storm is at least at tropical storm strength. The numbers are added together and then cubed.

"One of the most certain outcomes of global warming is a rise in sea level, caused both by the melting of ice and by thermal expansion of seawater."

Reliable, regular measurement of hurricane wind speeds has made the PDI a useful gauge of hurricane strength. These measurements show that hurricanes in the North Atlantic have become more energetic, with higher top wind speeds and longer duration. Whether these intensifying storms are the result of a natural cycle, or are worsening through the effects of an artificially warming atmosphere, is a debate that continues to divide meteorologists.

Wave Heights and Superstorms

Rising sea-surface temperatures are contributing to an era of more intense hurricane activity. Warmer water at the surface brings about more rapid evaporation, which contributes to the strength of tropical storms. At the same time, a rise in wave height is multiplying the effect of hurricanes on coastal areas.

An array of instruments now measure ocean wave height. Accelerometers measure the movement of buoys as underlying waves carry them up and down, from trough to crest. Pressure sensors measure the mass of water directly above them; the changes in pressure indicate the height of waves. Paul Komar and Jonathan Allan, two researchers in Oregon, have been measuring wave heights in the Pacific Ocean during the past three decades. They have found an average increase of 15.75 inches (40 cm) over that time, and also a rise of 2.75 inches (7 cm) in the average wave height of the five largest winter storms each year.[4]

Wave heights are increasing in the Atlantic Ocean as well. Greater wave height means stronger storm surges when hurricanes arrive at the shore. This brings more severe damage and flooding, and flooding of a larger inland area as levees break or are overrun and rivers bring a storm tide several hundred miles inland. Some scientists are warning of the approach of "super hurricanes," much larger and stronger storms that can affect several thousand miles of coastline.[5]

Hurricanes also multiply another important effect of global warming: a general rise in sea level. "One of the most certain outcomes of global warming is a rise in sea level, caused both by the melting of ice and by thermal expansion of seawater," comments Chris Mooney in *Storm World: Hurricanes, Politics, and the Battle over Global Warming,* "If all hurricanes ride atop higher seas, then barring some dramatic retreat from coastal areas, all hurricanes pose a greater threat to human lives and property in those areas—whether or not the storms have independently intensified."[6]

High-Risk Behavior

Risky behavior by humans contributes to hurricane damage. Coastal areas of the southeastern United States have seen rapid development. People are building new homes, hotels, resorts, and cities along seacoasts vulnerable to Atlantic storms. Emanuel comments that "by far the most important hurricane problem we face is demographic and political. Consider that Katrina, as horrible as it was, was by no means unprecedented, meteorologically speaking. More intense storms have struck the U.S. coastline long ago. The big problem is the headlong rush to tropical coastlines, coupled with federal and state policies that subsidize the risk incurred by coastal development."[7]

As Emanuel points out, since the 1960s the United States has been supporting this risky behavior. Standard home-insurance policies do not cover damages caused by flooding. Beginning in 1968, the National Flood Insurance Program began offering flood insurance to protect coastal homes against storm surges. The U.S. Congress created this program in the face of the rising costs of emergency assistance to natural-disaster areas. In return for making the insurance available, the twenty thousand communities covered by the program must take measures to protect themselves against storm damage.

To determine who must buy flood insurance, the federal government designates Special Flood Hazard Areas (SFHAs), based on the statistical probability that a damaging flood will affect the area. Before a home buyer can secure a loan to buy a property in an SFHA, he or she must purchase federal flood insurance, at an average cost in 2009 of about $500 in premiums a year. The policy covers losses up to $250,000.

For taxpayers, who ultimately pay for flood damage covered by this insurance, the risks (damages) aren't worth the reward (premiums). Realistically, the insurance should cost much more—several thousand dollars a year—to cover the risk. In addition, the availability of flood insurance to anyone willing to pay the minimal costs encourages further coastal development. As a result of the federal flood insurance program, massive coastal development in South Carolina, Florida, and other states has destroyed natural storm barriers, causing greater risk of flooding to communities located "safely" inland.[8]

Adapting to Hurricanes

As with other consequences of climate change, human societies will be forced to adapt to stronger and more frequent hurricanes.

This will mean zoning laws that restrict coastal development and changes in building codes to require the reinforcement of homes and buildings against high winds and storm surges. Disaster preparedness—the construction of shelters, for example—will have to improve in inland areas unaccustomed to hurricanes.

Another consideration is the artificial channeling of water in coastal areas and the destruction of wetlands and other natural barriers to tropical storms. Much of the damage caused by Hurricane Katrina was a result of human interference with the Louisiana coast and its complex system of mangroves, barrier islands, and tidal wetlands. When these barriers are destroyed by artificial channeling and development, hurricane storm surges reach farther inland and create more flooding and damage. Several projects designed to return the lower Mississippi River and its delta system to its natural state have been proposed.

In other nations, adaptation will mean a general migration away from coastal areas that become too hazardous to sustain permanent communities. *The Stern Review on the Economics of Climate Change*, a 700-page report by economist Nicholas Stern to the British government, spelled out the threat of storm surge to coastal plains around the world: "Currently more than 200 million people live in coastal floodplains around the world, with two million square kilometers of land and one trillion dollars worth of assets less than one metre elevation above current sea level . . . Many of the world's major cities (22 of the top 50) are at risk of flooding from coastal surges."[9] Like the hurricanes or tropical storms themselves, any mass movement of people inland will also cause disruption and do damage to the natural environment.

Notes

1. "3.2 Million Rendered Homeless by Nargis: Study" *Thaindian News*, May 15, 2008. www.thaindian.com.
2. Kevin Trenberth and Dennis Shea, "Atlantic Hurricanes and Natural Variability in 2005," *Geophysical Research Letters*, vol. 33, June 27, 2006.
3. Trenberth and Shea, "Atlantic Hurricanes and Natural Variability in 2005."
4. The Coastal Data Information Program, *Wave Measurement*, n.d. http://cdip.uscd.edu.

5. Stefan Rahmstorf et al., "Hurricanes and Global Warming—Is There a Connection?" *RealClimate*, September 2005. www.realclimate.com.

6. Chris Mooney, *Storm World: Hurricanes, Politics, and the Battle over Global Warming.* Orlando, FL: Harcourt, 2007, p. 165.

7. Kerry Emanuel, "Anthropogenic Effects on Tropical Cyclone Activity," January 2006. http://wind.mit.edu/~emanuel.

8. Scott E. Harrington, "Rethinking Disaster Policy: Breaking the Cycle of 'Free' Disaster Assistance, Subsidized Insurance, and Risky Behavior," *Regulation*, vol. 23, 2000, pp. 40–46.

9. Quoted in David Spratt and Philip Sutton, *Climate Code Red: The Case for Emergency Action.* Melbourne, Australia: Scribe, 2008, p. 42.

CHAPTER 6

Extratropical Storms

A n extratropical storm begins outside the tropics and gen-erally occurs between 30 and 60 degrees of latitude. These thunderstorms, tornadoes, hailstorms, and blizzards are the most costly weather events over inland regions.

Thunderstorms are the most common extratropical storm. At any one time, about 1,800 thunderstorms are occurring around the world.[1] They are spawned by low-pressure systems that give rise to cumulonimbus clouds, which tower fifty thousand feet—and higher—above the ground. The powerful jet streams meet these rising columns of water vapor, spreading the clouds hori-zontally and creating more atmospheric turbulence. When there is a sharp change in temperature as altitude increases, and heavy moisture present in the lower levels of the atmosphere, condi-tions are ripe for thunderstorms. The storms pick up energy from heat and moisture present at the surface. This connection is the reason, in many areas, thunderstorm activity peaks in the late afternoon and evening, when latent heat at ground level is at its strongest.

Thunderstorms are at their most dangerous as the super-cells that develop in the Great Plains and over the Appalachian Mountains. These are massive storm-spawning clouds that rise to as high as sixty thousand feet and remain stationary, pour-ing down rain, hail, and lightning and breeding strong winds and violent tornadoes. Conditions are good for supercells when cold air moving south from Canada and the Arctic meets warm tropical air from the Gulf of Mexico. This increases the instability of the air, while rapidly falling barometric pressure helps storm clouds to form. The southwest monsoon that pulls moist air from the Gulf of California across the Southwest during the summer also provides fertile ground for developing thunderstorms, supercells, and tornadoes.

Tornadoes and Global Warming

Meteorologists are still learning about tornadoes. They know that several ingredients are necessary for the creation of these powerful windstorms. There must be clouds and atmospheric instability, as well as lift and wind shear. An increase in CO_2 levels may also be playing a new role. An index known as the Convective Available Potential Energy (CAPE) scale measures wind shear between the ground and a height of 3.7 miles (6 km) in the atmosphere. The higher the CAPE reading, generally, the more likely tornadoes are to form. In one climate model, a doubling of the CO_2 levels in the atmosphere would bring a higher CAPE reading, and thus the more likely chance of severe weather.[2]

Tornadoes are measured on the Enhanced Fujita Scale, a newer version of the Fujita scale, which since 2007 classifies these storms on a scale of EF0 to EF5. The Fujita scales measure tornado strength according to the amount of damage the storm causes, not according to its wind speed (which in most cases cannot be directly measured). Most of the damage is caused by the worst tornadoes: the rare EF4 and EF5 storms that can bring catastrophic damage and heavy loss of life. Although the number of tornadoes has increased since the 1950s, the number of exceptionally strong storms has remained fairly constant. Between 1992 and 1999, there were six F5 tornadoes in the United States. Since 2007 only one EF5 storm was recorded in the United States, and one in Canada.

Nevertheless, a chart of the occurrence of tornadoes since 1950 shows in convincing detail that overall tornado frequency

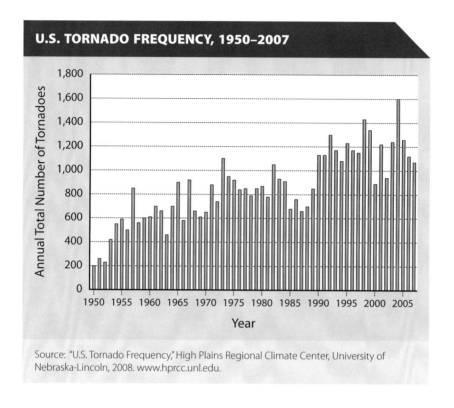

U.S. TORNADO FREQUENCY, 1950–2007

Source: "U.S. Tornado Frequency," High Plains Regional Climate Center, University of Nebraska-Lincoln, 2008. www.hprcc.unl.edu.

is increasing. A more active hydrologic cycle may be contributing to instability in the upper atmosphere that leads to tornadoes, hailstorms, and other damaging weather. But there could be other factors involved, arising from the very brief history of climate recordkeeping.

Most tornadoes are brief, local events. In the past, most occurred without any human witnesses. The settlement of the Great Plains and the rise in population throughout tornado-prone areas of the United States brought about more reporting. More tornadoes and extreme weather are now seen, and so more tornadoes seem to be occurring. In addition, new Doppler radar deployed by weather forecasters allows meteorologists to track and record all, not just some, of the heavy storm cells that give birth to tornadoes. Tornado science has advanced in another important way in the past few decades—a single storm giving rise

Although the strength of individual tornadoes cannot be attributed to global warming, some observers do link the storms' growing frequency to climate change. AP Images.

to multiple tornadoes along a track of damage might once have been classified as a single, extremely damaging tornado; now it goes into the records as multiple occurrences.

The Northward Storm Track

There are other variables involved in the frequency of tornadoes. Global warming may be contributing to the incidence of tornadoes by increasing atmospheric instability. Meteorologists have spotted a significant trend in recent years that has a direct bearing on the occurrence of extratropical storms and tornadoes. The general track of thunderstorms has been moving northward in the Atlantic and Pacific oceans, as has the location of the polar jet stream. This mass of upper-level air is moved about by the pressure and temperature gradients between the equator and the polar latitudes. A warming of sea-surface temperatures in the tropics tends to push the jet stream northward and create more atmospheric turbulence in the mid-latitudes. The faster the changes in temperature and pressure, the steeper the gradient, and the more latent energy that is available to storm systems.

Climate-change observers believe that a northward shifting storm track may bring more tornadoes to the plains of central Canada. In addition, with a change of seasons and a warmer spring, tornado season may begin earlier in the year. Another consequence of warming, however, is a reduced amount of wind shear, which would tend to reduce the intensity of storms. The 2007 report by the Intergovernmental Panel on Climate Change (IPCC) concludes that "There is insufficient evidence to determine whether trends exist in small-scale phenomena such as tornadoes, hail, lighting, and dust storms."[3]

> *The higher atmospheric turbulence caused by an intensified hydrologic cycle around the world . . . should bring a higher incidence of thunderstorms. These conditions could also usher in a more common occurrence of one of the most damaging weather events of all: the superstorm.*

As dangerous and damaging as they can be, tornadoes remain local, insignificant events on a global meteorological scale. No single occurrence of a heavy storm, even an EF5 tornado or a powerful hurricane, can be directly attributed to climate change or global warming. Although satellite readings and Doppler radar allow weather bureaus to track storms with greater accuracy, meteorological data remains inconclusive on the possibility that the number of thunderstorms and hailstorms has been increasing in recent decades.

The Superstorms

Although the records are still scanty, the higher atmospheric turbulence caused by an intensified hydrologic cycle around the world—which also brings a higher amount of water vapor

The Enhanced Fujita Scale

The Fujita scale was named for Tetsuya Theodore "Ted" Fujita, a physicist at the University of Chicago who was one of the world's first tornado specialists. To devise his measurement of the strongest storms on Earth, Fujita tracked data on tornadoes and the damage they wrought back to 1916, and he traveled throughout the Great Plains and the Midwest to personally survey the damage caused by tornadoes. The scale, which rated tornadoes on a scale of F0 to F5, was replaced in 2007 by the Enhanced Fujita Scale; it now classifies tornadoes as EF0 through EF5. The scale remains the only dependable way to measure tornado strength; even if instrumentation were coincidentally to be positioned in the path of a tornado, most devices cannot withstand tornadic winds. Top winds of an EF5 reach more than 200 miles (322 km) per hour, blowing homes off their foundations. Although former F5, and now EF5, tornadoes are rare (there were a total of fifty-one official F5 tornadoes recorded from 1953 to 2007, and only two EF5 tornadoes have been recorded since 2007), meteorologists are considering the possibility that in the future global warming could bring superstorms to the Great Plains and tornadoes with winds that could exceed this scale's top ranking.

and higher relative humidity—should bring a higher incidence of thunderstorms. These conditions could also usher in a more common occurrence of one of the most damaging weather events of all: the superstorm.

The eastern seaboard of the United States has been home to some of the most extreme extratropical weather experienced in the northern hemisphere. On October 28, 1991, a cold front off the Atlantic coasts of Canada and the United States moved into the waters off Nova Scotia, and began to gather tropical air from a hurricane spinning near the island of Bermuda. The low-pressure system developed into a monster storm and returned to the southwest, clashing with a high-pressure front over eastern Canada. Winds intensified to 70 miles (113 km) per hour, wave heights reached 40 feet (12 m), and the East Coast of the United States was pounded by a storm front that extended for more than 1,000 miles (1,609 km). Wind records were shattered from Massachusetts to the Outer Banks of North Carolina. Coastal flooding was extensive—but the storm was not yet finished. Moving farther south, the front met the Gulf Stream and warm tropical waters, which provided even more fuel for what was now a full-fledged hurricane. Ranging over nearly half the length of the Atlantic coast, the system was officially named The Perfect Storm by the National Weather Service.

The Superstorm of 1993 was the most powerful blizzard of the twentieth century, and the most intense extratropical storm ever to occur on the eastern seaboard of the United States. The storm began to develop in the Gulf of Mexico, moving up the Atlantic coast and bringing heavy snow across the eastern half of the country, from Alabama to New York. The lowest barometric pressure in history was recorded at dozens of locations in the Appalachian region. Tornadoes plowed across Florida, which experienced a record cold front. The storm closed every major airport on the East Coast, and caused heavy damage to overhead power lines, which in some places cut electricity for a week or longer.

These superstorms are not limited to North America. The continent of Europe is prone to heavy extratropical storms brought by westerly winds during the winter months. A severe storm brought winds of more than 175 miles (280 km) per hour to the North Sea coasts in 1953. The storm surge and flooding drowned more than two thousand people in the Netherlands and overwhelmed the dikes meant to protect that low-lying country from the sea. On the night of October 15, 1987, a powerful windstorm struck Great Britain, blowing down thousands of trees in London parks. Another superstorm reached the continent in 1999, with France hit by winds exceeding 100 miles (160 km) per hour and the Alps region suffering major blizzards and deadly avalanches. Heavy storms during the summer of 2002 in central Europe caused a wave of river flooding that inundated hundreds of cities and caused more than one hundred deaths.

A Stormy Future

Recent decades have seen a decline in the number of snowstorms in the southern and midwestern United States, and an increase in the Northeast and the Upper Midwest. The northward-shifting storm track is responsible, along with the sharper pressure and temperature gradients measured in the middle latitudes. A 2007 study by Jeff Yin of the National Center for Atmospheric Research examined fifteen advanced global climate models. Yin's conclusion was that extratropical storms will be shifting northward and undergoing an increase in their intensity.[4]

With continued atmospheric warming, meteorologists expect more rapid evaporation from the surface and a higher water-vapor content in the air. The result will be higher humidity readings, more atmospheric instability, and more abundant fuel for the development of thunderstorms, supercells, and tornadoes. Stronger and more frequent thunderstorms, stronger tornadoes, and more frequent blizzards are the likely results.

Notes

1. H. Michael Mogil, *Extreme Weather: Understanding the Science of Hurricanes, Tornadoes, Floods, Heat Waves, Snow Storms, Global Warming, and Other Atmospheric Disturbances*. New York: Black Dog and Leventhal, 2007, p. 135.
2. Anthony Del Genio and Joanna Futyan, "Deep Convective System Evolution Over Africa and the Tropical Atlantic," *Journal of Climate*, vol. 20, October 15, 2007.
3. S. Solomon et al., eds., "Summary for Policymakers," in *Climate Change 2007: The Physical Science Basis. Contribution of Working Group I to the Fourth Assessment Report of the Intergovernmental Panel on Climate Change*. Cambridge and New York: Cambridge University Press, 2007.
4. Robert Henson, *The Rough Guide to Climate Change*. London and New York: Rough Guides, 2006, pp. 132–33.

CHAPTER 7

Seasonal Variability

The winter is a busy weather time in the Rocky Mountains. Heavy storms pound the slopes, burying forests of aspen and pine in powdery snow. By November, conditions in Colorado, Utah, and Wyoming are just right for a smooth, fast run down the mountainsides on a pair of skis or a snowboard.

In recent years, however, a change has occurred in the mountainous West. The ski season and seasonal weather have become unpredictable. Some resorts have to use snow machines to get any snow on the ground at all. Winters have become warmer and drier, and in general the cold weather arrives later in the year. Spring comes earlier and brings with it warmer temperatures and fewer spring snowstorms. Without a predictable snow season, ski resorts can't sell lift tickets or rooms in advance. There has been a subtle shift in the duration and nature of the seasons—a predicted result of global warming.

Snow reliability—the probability that a certain area will have enough snow for winter recreation—is a crucial ingredient for the success of a tourism-dependent economy in mountain regions of Colorado, as well as Alpine regions of Austria and Switzerland. A 2006 study by researchers at the United Nations Environmental

Following page: Increasing cases of dengue fever and other vector-borne diseases in India may be tied directly to increasing amounts of precipitation there. Raveendran/AFP/Getty Images.

Programme noted that as temperatures rise, snow reliability falls, and that "climate change is a severe threat to snow-related sports such as skiing, snowboarding and cross-country skiing . . . the ski tourism industry will climb up the mountains to reach snow-reliable areas at high altitude. This process will lead to a concentration of winter sport activities, and will put further pressure on the sensitive environment of high mountains."[1]

Global Warming and Seasonal Variation

The annual change in seasonal weather is a familiar aspect of climate for most people on Earth. These seasonal changes are caused by regular changes in the position of the earth relative to the sun as the planet travels its 365-day orbit. Because the earth is tilted along its polar axis at an angle of 23.5 degrees to its orbital plane, the northern and southern hemispheres do not receive the same amount of solar radiation at any one time. When the northern hemisphere is tilted more directly toward the sun, for example, hours of daylight over this half of the earth are longer and the intensity of solar radiation is higher. When the northern hemisphere is tilted away, the days are shorter and sunlight is less intense. The results, respectively, are summer and winter.

In a single location, changing seasons bring weather changes. Humidity, barometric pressure, and precipitation all vary from one season to the next. In the middle latitudes, and in regions far from the moderating winds and currents of the sea, a continental climate brings more extreme changes from winter to summer. In the tropics, where the received solar radiation is more constant throughout the year, the difference in seasons may be slight.

Several theories exist concerning the effect of global warming on the length and characteristics of the seasons. A rise in mean global temperature may bring longer and more humid summers, shorter and drier winters, and a change in the length of the fall and spring. There has been no systematic measurement of seasonal temperatures or other aspects, however—only scattered evidence showing that in the past few decades the seasons have indeed been changing.

Changing season length brings new challenges. Growing seasons will change for farmers. Some of their crops may flourish under the new conditions while others suffer and prove unable to cope with the changing environment. Livestock herds could also be affected by longer, more arid summers that dry up their pastures. Harvests that depend entirely on seasonal weather will be the most drastically affected. One example is the annual spring collection of maple syrup, which has been carried out for centuries in New England. According to the U.S. National Assessment of Climate Change, "To produce the best syrup, maples need a series of freezing nights and milder days, together with a few prolonged cold snaps in late winter. But since the 1980s, winters across New England haven't lived up to their past performance. There have been fewer stretches of bitter cold, and nights are staying above freezing more often, even in midwinter."[2]

A change in season length would change migration patterns for species that move with the coming of winter and spring. In search of food and shelter, many species in mountainous locations simply change their elevation. Others use flyways or familiar river routes to move much greater distances, in some cases from one continent to another. The disruption of migratory patterns could effect a chain reaction, as needed food sources move or disappear. If a particular location experiences a sustained rise in winter temperatures, some species may cease migrating altogether. "Hidden in the world of plants and animals is a great deal of synchronicity," comment the authors of *Climate: The Force That Shapes Our World*. "Organisms that rely on others for food, pollination, or other resources and services—that is to say, most plants and animals—depend on the others being available when and where they need them. This synchronicity is being lost as climate changes."[3]

Seasonal change also affects vector-borne diseases that are brought from place to place by a host or carrier (such as the tropical disease malaria and the mosquito). The problem is unpredictability. Not knowing with confidence the date of arrival of a dry or rainy season, for example, a national health service cannot prepare for the regular arrival of water-borne diseases. Typhoid, dengue fever, malaria, and other illnesses are appearing in new places and affecting a greater range of population.

One Indian health official, Sukumar Devotta, explains to a reporter for the *Times of India* that "the amount of rain may not have increased substantially, but surely the amount of precipitation (maybe in lesser days) is increasing. Similarly, drought conditions are also on the rise. It rains for fewer days but much more heavily, causing floods. These have increased the cases of vector-borne diseases like malaria, dengue, chikungunya and water-borne diseases like typhoid, jaundice, diarrhoea, gastroenteritis etc. on one hand and also diseases like respiratory disorders due to bad air quality in dry weather on the other hand."[4]

Also, the range of a disease-carrying insect could move northward if winter temperatures rise and killing frosts become less common. New diseases are reaching into India, such as Japanese encephalitis, the Chandipura virus, and chikungunya. If the seasons significantly change, these problems will most strongly affect areas already struggling with drought, famine, stronger storms, and flooding.

Foliation: A Key Indicator of Seasonal Variation

Changes in temperature and season length bring a series of physical changes to the natural environment. In the deciduous forests of North America, Siberia, and central Europe, for example, scientists have been using satellite imagery and simple, ground-based record-keeping to study the spring appearance of new leaves (foliation), which depends largely on temperature.

Warming trends took place in the late 1930s and early 1940s, bringing earlier foliation during these years; from 1945 until 1960, temperatures cooled and new leaves appeared later in the spring. The early 1980s again saw lower spring temperatures and late foliation, whereas in the 1990s spring temperatures were consistently higher and foliation took place at the earliest dates since the 1920s. Since 1982, foliation has taken place, on average, five days earlier in the northern forests of Europe and Siberia.

Siberia and northern North America are regions especially vulnerable to seasonal shifts. As warmer seasons lengthen and

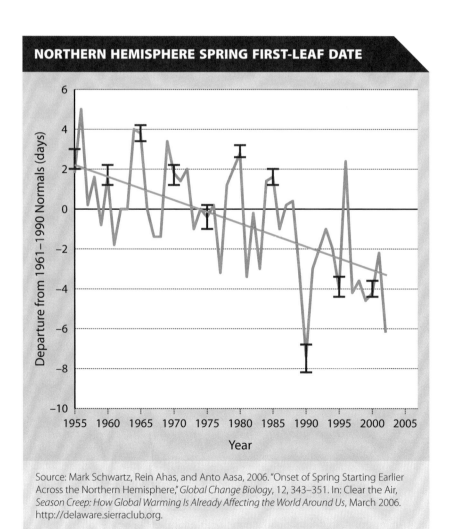

NORTHERN HEMISPHERE SPRING FIRST-LEAF DATE

Source: Mark Schwartz, Rein Ahas, and Anto Aasa, 2006. "Onset of Spring Starting Earlier Across the Northern Hemisphere," *Global Change Biology*, 12, 343–351. In: Clear the Air, *Season Creep: How Global Warming Is Already Affecting the World Around Us*, March 2006. http://delaware.sierraclub.org.

winters grow shorter, the forest itself may shift northward, into regions previously covered by tundra and permafrost. To the south, regions of prairie may replace the coniferous forest now growing in the Upper Midwest and southern Canada. The number of frost days could decrease, while the total amount of cultivable land in these regions would rise—on a local level, a beneficial effect of warming. "Global agricultural productivity is predicted to go *up* during the next century," comments author Robert Henson in *The Rough Guide to Climate Change*, "thanks to the extra CO_2 in the atmosphere and now-barren regions becoming warm enough to bear crops. However, the rich world looks to reap the benefits: Crop yields in the tropics, home to hundreds of millions of subsistence farmers, are likely to drop."[5]

Dhaka will be prone to annual superflooding that could cause a wave of climate refugees throughout Bangladesh and south Asia.

Wherever they occur, seasonal variations and changes will have a strong impact on agriculture. In some scenarios, where growing seasons lengthen, crop yields will increase and prices will fall. Climate-change observers have also predicted a rise in prices and a fall in yields as drought becomes more extensive and damaging. The key for farmers and livestock herders is adaptation to the changing natural environment and seasons. The changes may lead to investment in new seed varieties, the adoption of new planting and harvest schedules, and changes in land use.

Wealthier societies, which are largely responsible for the emission of greenhouse gases into the atmosphere, will be better equipped to make these adaptations. Poorer countries may see their farming sectors hard-pressed to provide necessary food. Having less developed industry, these societies have contributed less, proportionally, than richer countries have to the greenhouse problem. But most of them are in latitudes and locations that will be more directly affected by changes in important seasonal events, such as the annual monsoons of south Asia.

The Seasonal Monsoon

The monsoons of tropical Asia and Africa are essential to food production in these regions. But changes in deep-ocean currents around the world are affecting the monsoons. In the Atlantic Ocean, warming sea temperatures reduce the amount of sinking cold water that gives rise to the Gulf Stream current. The Gulf Stream is an important part of the global conveyer of ocean currents that links the North and South Atlantic, the Indian Ocean, and the Pacific Ocean. If this system changes in a significant way, the tropical monsoons that bring essential rain to south Asia may be shortened or interrupted.

Seasonal changes in the monsoon have already begun. The annual monsoon is beginning later than usual in Mexico and in southwestern North America, bringing fewer days of rain and drought conditions. At the same time, storms that do occur tend to be heavier, causing flash flooding, heavy damage, and loss of life in especially arid or drought-stricken areas.

Reduced rainfall during a shortened monsoon season will not lessen flooding in places such as Dhaka, Bangladesh. In this crowded city, increased spring snowmelt from the Himalaya Mountains to the north threatens catastrophic urban floods. Lying between 10 feet and 23 feet (3 m and 7 m) above sea level, Dhaka was built at the confluence of three major rivers: the Ganges, the Brahmaputra, and the Meghna. Together, these three streams carry 35 trillion cubic feet of water downstream every year to the Bay of Bengal. If warmer weather in the mountains brings regular, heavier snowmelt and spring runoff, the city and the river deltas to the south will be prone to annual superflooding that could cause a wave of climate refugees throughout Bangladesh and south Asia.[6]

El Niño

An important part of any climate change scenario is a shift in El Niño, a naturally occurring variation that affects climate in much of the western hemisphere. Also known as the El Niño-Southern Oscillation (ENSO), this warming trend occurs in the waters of the eastern Pacific Ocean. A vast current of water travels across the Pacific, eventually reaching the western shores of South America. Every few years, El Niño causes important seasonal shifts throughout the western hemisphere, affecting rainfall, drought, and storminess in the United States.

El Niño has been studied since the late nineteenth century. It was originally named for the Christmas season in which its effects are strongest (El Niño means "the boy," or the Christ child, in Spanish). A strong El Niño event began in 1982; the most recent began in 1997. In late 2009, warmer ocean temperature readings hinted that the next El Niño was about to arrive. A related La Niña also occurs on a regular basis, following the end of El Niño. La Niña is an upwelling of cold water in the tropical Pacific, which brings drier and warmer weather to North America and cooler, wetter weather to Southeast Asia.

Off the Peruvian coast of South America, El Niño brings warmer waters and an increase in the number of tropical cyclones. Hurricanes fueled by the warm waters develop in tropical latitudes and move toward Mexico and North America (the southerly jet stream during an El Niño also disrupts hurricane formation in the Atlantic Ocean). Important consequences occur over land, including heavier rains, stronger thunderstorms, and flooding that affects arid regions of western South America as well as Mexico and the southwestern United States. El Niño also intensifies drought conditions in Australia and Southeast Asia.

A global rise in sea-surface temperatures may be strengthening El Niño. Since 1976, there have been a total of seven El Niño events, whereas normally in that span of time only five would have been expected. This shift could be a result of rising average temperatures in the tropics and around the world.

The Real Danger: A Stronger La Niña

The El Niño phenomenon, a part of the natural seesaw in barometric pressure known as the Southern Oscillation, is well known for bringing warmer waters to the eastern Pacific and storms to the southwestern United States; few meteorologists have much to say about La Niña, except as an aside. But a strengthening La Niña current could have much more serious consequences. "If the La Niña event is strong enough to affect the jet streams," warns an online report from The GLOBE Program, "its effects are often more volatile than El Niño's. For example, while El Niño–influenced jet stream patterns often help keep hurricanes away from the eastern coast of the United States, hurricanes during La Niña could become more frequent and intense."

From 1998 through 2002, a full five years of cooler-than-normal temperatures took place in the waters off South America. Not coincidentally, high-pressure zones developed at 40 degrees of latitude in both hemispheres, causing droughts in North America, Australia, and Asia. Computer modeling shows that, with rising sea-surface temperatures in the western Pacific, strengthening trade winds blowing toward the west cause further upwelling of deep, cold water off South America. The cold La Niña waters rise and spread, contributing to the chain reaction that eventually brings persistent high pressure and drought to the landmasses bordering the Pacific.

In the last few decades, La Niña has been strengthening and is now threatening to dominate the El Niño current if global temperatures continue to rise. La Niña may be the primary reason droughts have become longer and more severe around the world, and it may prove the most serious danger to agriculture and water supplies in affected nations.

The increasingly warm waters off the Peruvian coast will affect thousands of miles of natural habitat on which fishing industries depend. Heavier storms may also result in the U.S.

Southwest, where drought conditions heighten the danger of flash flooding.

El Niño is one of many examples of natural variances in the global climate that are undergoing transformation in an era of anthropogenic global warming. These changes will demand adaptation by human societies directly affected by them, as the measures to combat global warming remain controversial, expensive and—so far—ineffective in reversing the unpredictable and dangerous trend.

Notes

1. Bruno Abegg, Rolf Burki, and Hans Elsasser, "Climate Change and Winter Sports: Environmental and Economic Threats," United Nations Environment Programme, November 19, 2006. www.viewsfromtheworld.com.
2. Robert Henson, *The Rough Guide to Climate Change*, London and New York: Rough Guides, 2006, p. 152.
3. Jennifer Hoffman, Tina Tin, and George Ochoa, *Climate: The Force That Shapes Our World and the Future of Life on Earth*. Emmaus, PA: Rodale, 2005, p. 174.
4. Quoted in Snehlata Shrivastav, "Global Warming, Health Warning." http://timesof indiaindiatimes.com.
5. Henson, *The Rough Guide to Climate Change*, n.d., p. 14.
6. Roger Harrabin, "Climate Fears for Bangladesh's Future," BBC.com, September 14, 2006. http://news.bbc.co.uk.

CHAPTER 8

Conclusion

Does anthropogenic, or human-induced, global warming threaten a new climate era of increased storminess and extreme weather such as massive hurricanes, stronger tornadoes, heavier rains, killer floods, drought, and other natural disasters as yet unforeseen? As with many other questions related to global warming, this one remains unanswered, and a subject of ongoing debate—as uncertain as a daily weather forecast.

In this debate, however, a few significant numbers stand out. The earth has warmed 1.33°F (.74°C) during the twentieth century, a rate faster than in the past. The level of carbon dioxide in the atmosphere has risen from 280 parts per million to about 380 parts per million in the last two centuries. The increasing carbon dioxide is largely due to the burning of fossil fuels during the industrial age. Carbon dioxide and other greenhouse gases have the effect of warming temperatures over land and sea. During the next fifty years, taking the accelerating rise in CO_2 levels into account, the earth could warm another 2°F–3°F (1.1°C–1.7°C). The result would be higher sea-surface temperatures that contribute to stronger weather systems that fuel hurricanes and tropical cyclones. Increasing evaporation and atmospheric water vapor in the atmosphere would also intensify the hydrologic cycle, which brings water from the seas to the skies and back to the surface.

A further rise in temperature at its current rate over the next fifty years could have significant impacts on the global economy and on living conditions for people around the world. Rising sea levels, caused by melting polar ice caps, could flood densely inhabited coastal zones. The impact could be especially severe for Southeast Asia, the Pacific Ocean islands, the Caribbean islands, and for large coastal cities including Tokyo, Shanghai, New York, London, Miami, St. Petersburg, Mumbai, Calcutta, and Buenos Aires. It could also damage important infrastructure, such as oil refineries, nuclear power stations, ports, and industrial facilities that are located near coastal area.

A more intense hydrologic cycle would bring extreme weather with greater frequency and intensity. Peak wind speeds of tropical storms would rise, causing greater damage and loss of life. Hurricanes and their storm surges are already the most costly natural disasters known. A shift in monsoon seasons, and in the El Niño phenomenon, would seriously affect agriculture and water supplies in North and South America. Areas now going through severe drought, such as the western United States and southeastern Australia, would turn into arid deserts with limited capacity to sustain settlement or cities of any size.

Catastrophic floods and droughts could create new disease vectors—pathways for the transmission of malaria, cholera, and other serious illnesses. More frequent heat waves would cause widespread misery, forest fires, drought, and heat-related deaths. The distribution of animal species could change, and flora and fauna would face an increasing threat of extinction when species are unable to adapt.

Humans would face severe shortages of water in areas affected by drought. In drought-stricken areas, natural spring snowmelt would be reduced, affecting the ability of farmers to cultivate crops. Many regions could enter a new era of scarce water, in which this resource would be rationed by public authorities. Africa, the Middle East, southern Europe, the western

United States, and drier regions of Central and South America could experience long-term drought conditions.

The ability to adapt has allowed the human race to survive and dominate the natural environment of planet Earth—to the extent that human activity is now having an effect on global climate. Humans will have to draw on this adapting skill if climate change continues and intensifies. Regions once home to large concentrations of people in cities may have to be abandoned, and new areas may have to be settled. New methods of preserving water for agriculture, irrigation, and household use will have to be invented. Coastal populations will have to protect themselves against flooding by raising seawalls and creating flood diversions. Health-care systems must prepare for the spread of tropical diseases into areas where they were once unknown.

Many scientists are now warning of climate tipping points, at which drastic and damaging effects of warming will become inevitable. At a certain global average temperature, for example, the melting of polar ice caps will begin to accelerate, causing a rise in sea level that will flood every major city located on a seacoast. To avoid a future tipping point, humans must find a way to control or slow down greenhouse-gas emissions. They can do so by an international agreement, by new technology that lessens the need to burn fossil fuels, or by a combination of both. Although it is the easiest option, inaction on climate change is also the most dangerous.

Glossary

anthropogenic Caused by humans.

Atlantic Multidecadal Oscillation (AMO) A cycle of tropical depressions and storm formation in the mid-Atlantic Ocean.

Coriolis effect The rotation of air and water under the influence of the earth's rotation.

desertification The transformation of productive land to arid and infertile desert through a general fall in annual precipitation.

disease vector A method for the transportation of disease by a host from one place to the next, such as the spread of malaria by mosquitoes.

El Niño A cyclical warming of the Pacific Ocean's eastern waters that causes changes in climate patterns in the western hemisphere.

Enhanced Fujita Scale A scale for measuring the strength of tornadic winds based on the amount of damage they cause.

extratropical storm A large storm system that arises outside of the tropical regions.

extreme weather A weather event, such as a heat wave or rainfall, that is at the extremes of historical distribution, such as one that falls within the highest or lowest 10 percent of the extreme measurements experienced in a single location.

feedback loop A process in which one condition creates other conditions that reinforce the first.

General Circulation Model (GCM) A computer model of future climate patterns that draws on a variety of inputs, including a rise in greenhouse-gas concentrations.

greenhouse effect Warming of the atmosphere by increased concentration of heat-trapping gases, such as carbon dioxide.

greenhouse gas A compound that traps solar radiation in Earth's atmosphere.

Gulf Stream An ocean current that warms the North Atlantic Ocean and continental Europe.

hydrologic cycle The natural process of evaporation from the sea surface and subsequent precipitation from the atmosphere.

Intergovernmental Panel on Climate Change (IPCC) A climate-study group organized under the authority of the United Nations, which issues regular reports on trends in global climate.

jet stream A high-level atmospheric current that plays an important role in the speed and direction of weather systems.

La Niña A cyclical cooling of the waters of the eastern Pacific Ocean.

Milankovitch cycles Gradual changes in Earth's orbit and rotation that, in combination, affect the global climate.

monsoon A seasonal period of rain, cool temperatures, and wind that occurs in tropical regions throughout the world.

ozone A gas consisting of three oxygen atoms. In the stratosphere, ozone protects the earth from harmful radiation; in the troposphere, ozone is a dangerous pollutant causing serious human illness and distress.

sea-surface temperature Water temperatures measured at the surface of the ocean.

stratosphere The atmospheric layer beginning about nine miles above the earth's surface and extending up to fourteen miles high.

thermohaline circulation The system of deep underwater currents that cycles ocean water from one region of the globe to the next.

troposphere The lowest portion of the atmosphere, extending up to nine miles above the surface of the earth.

wind shear High-level, multidirectional winds that tend to disrupt organized storm systems such as hurricanes.

For Further Research

Books

Dennis T. Avery and J. Fred Singer, *Unstoppable Global Warming Every 1,500 Years*. Lanham, MD: Rowman & Littlefield, 2007.
> The authors believe that a natural 1,500-year solar cycle is responsible for current temperature trends.

Tim Flannery, *The Weather Makers: How Man Is Changing the Climate and What It Means for Life on Earth*. Boston: Atlantic Monthly Press, 2006.
> A paleontologist examines the problem of climate change and maintains that rising CO_2 levels pose an imminent threat to the environment.

Ross Gelbspan, *Boiling Point: How Politicians, Big Oil and Coal, Journalists, and Activists Have Fueled a Climate Crisis—And What We Can Do to Avert Disaster*. New York: Basic Books, 2005.
> The author lays out a course of action to deal with the climate crisis, including tighter emission standards and the development of renewable and alternative energy sources.

———, *The Heat Is On: The Climate Crisis, the Cover-Up, the Prescription*. New York: Basic Books, 1998.
> The author believes a conspiracy among corporations and politicians is blocking much-needed action on climate change.

Al Gore, *Earth in the Balance: Ecology and the Human Spirit*. Emmaus, PA: Rodale Books, 2006.
> The author's take on the world's various environmental issues and the steps needed to solve them.

———, *An Inconvenient Truth: The Planetary Emergency of Global Warming and What We Can Do About It*. Emmaus, PA: Rodale Books, 2006.
> A best-selling book by the former U.S. vice president on the immediate threats posed by global warming.

Robert Henson, *The Rough Guide to Climate Change,* 2nd ed. London and New York: Rough Guides, 2008.
> An updated edition of a thoroughly researched guide to climate change that offers the reader a number of scientific theories, explanations, and projections.

Jennifer Hoffman, Tina Tin, and George Ochoa, *Climate: The Force That Shapes Our World and the Future of Life on Earth.* Emmaus, PA: Rodale Books, 2005.
> A book describing the various manifestation of Earth's climate system, with a fully illustrated chapter on extreme weather events.

John Houghton, *Global Warming: The Complete Briefing*, 3rd ed. Cambridge: Cambridge University Press, 2004.
> In detail, this illustrated book explains the science of global warming and the prospects for reversing it.

Elizabeth Kolbert, *Field Notes from a Catastrophe: Man, Nature, and Climate Change.* New York: Bloomsbury USA, 2006.
> Blaming politicians and voters for negligent inaction, the author calls for immediate steps to combat global warming.

Eugene Linden, *The Winds of Change: Climate, Weather, and the Destruction of Civilizations.* New York: Simon and Schuster, 2007.
> The author believes that a current era of benign climate is coming to an end, and that human society is facing a much more hostile climate environment in the future.

Bjorn Lomborg, *Cool It: The Skeptical Environmentalist's Guide to Global Warming.* New York: Vintage Books, 2008.
> A Danish author lays out a case for rational, incremental solutions to global warming, which he ranks relatively low as an imminent threat to global society.

James Lovelock, *The Revenge of Gaia: Earth's Climate Crisis and the Fate of Humanity.* New York: Basic Books, 2007.
> The author believes that Earth's self-regulating environmental system will soon make the planet hostile to human life, and believes that nuclear power is the most effective solution to the global warming problem.

Mark Lynas, *High Tide: The Truth About Our Climate Crisis.* New York: Picador, 2004.
> The author travels around the world to investigate the impact of global warming on the lives of everyday people.

———, *Six Degrees: Our Future on a Hotter Planet.* Washington, DC: National Geographic, 2008.
> The author details the consequences of global warming as currently projected by computer models and climate scientists.

Mark Maslin, *Global Warming: A Very Short Introduction.* New York: Oxford University Press, 2009.
> A book introducing the most important aspects of the subject of climate change, including political and scientific controversy and possible solutions.

H. Michael Mogil, *Extreme Weather: Understanding the Science of Hurricanes, Tornadoes, Floods, Heat Waves, Snow Storms, Global Warming, and Other Atmospheric Disturbances.* New York: Black Dog and Leventhal, 2007.
> The author offers a straightforward explanation of the causes of tornadoes, hurricanes, floods, droughts, and other extreme weather events.

Fred Pearce, *With Speed and Violence: Why Scientists Fear Tipping Points in Climate Change.* Boston: Beacon Press, 2007.
> The author illustrates the possible, very sudden consequences of a continued rise in global temperatures and "tipping points," from the melting of polar ice caps to the shutdown of the Asian monsoon.

James Gustave Speth, *Red Sky at Morning: America and the Crisis of the Global Environment.* New Haven, CT: Yale University Press, 2005.
> The author investigates the root causes of the environmental crisis, which he identifies as uncontrolled consumption, population growth, and technology.

David Spratt and Philip Sutton. *Climate Code Red: The Case for Emergency Action.* Melbourne, Australia: Scribe, 2008.
> The authors view the climate situation as a pressing emergency and propose immediate action to stem the threats of global warming.

Michael Tennesen, *The Complete Idiot's Guide to Global Warming*. New York: Alpha Books, 2008.

> The second, revised edition of an introductory book on the subject, useful for those who are investigating climate change for the first time.

Periodicals

Alun Anderson, "The Great Melt: The Coming Transformation of the Arctic," *World Policy Journal*, Winter 2009.

David S. Battisti and Rosamond L. Naylor, "Historical Warnings of Future Food Insecurity with Unprecedented Seasonal Heat," *Science*, January 9, 2009, p. 240.

Sharon Begley, "True or False: Global Warming Is a Cause of This Year's Extreme Weather," *Newsweek*, July 14, 2008, p. 52.

Ben Block, "Climate Change Will Worsen Hunger, Study Says," *Worldwatch*, January/February 2010.

———, "Public Health Leaders Stress Climate Risk," *Worldwatch*, September/October 2009.

Jamais Cascio, "Last-Resort Solutions to Global Warming: Geoengineering the Planet to Stave off Disaster," *The Futurist*, May-June 2009.

Jessica Cheng, "Global Warming: Not So Bad? Birds and Power Companies Adapt to Climate Change; Scientists Downgrade Its Role in Hurricane Formation," *Popular Science*, August 2008.

The Economist, "Off-Base Camp: Glaciers and the IPCC," January 23, 2010.

Indur M. Goklany, "Deaths and Death Rates from Extreme Weather Events: 1900–2008," *Journal of American Physicians and Surgeons*, December 22, 2009.

Alan Gomez, "Weather Extremes Stalk Each Coast," *USA Today*, June 17, 2009.

James Hansen, "A Gross Failure of Leadership," *Newsweek International*, December 14, 2009.

Darrell S. Kaufman et al., "Recent Warming Reverses Long-Term Arctic Cooling," *Science*, September 4, 2009.

Lonny Lippsett, "Ocean Conveyor's 'Pump' Switches Back On," *Oceanus*, Woods Hole Oceanographic Institute, www.whoi .edu/oceanus/viewArticle.do?id=54347.

Scott Loarie and Christopher Field, "Making the Paper: Can Plants and Animals Keep Pace with Changing Climates and Habitats?" *Nature*, December 31, 2009.

Robert Draper, "Australia's Dry Run," *National Geographic*, April 2009.

Nature, "Meteorology: Can't Beat the Heat," November 26, 2009.

Hubert Quetelard et al., "World-Record Rainfalls During Tropical Cyclone Gamede," *Bulletin of the American Meteorological Society*, May 2009.

Robert Repetto, "Changing Climate, More Damaging Weather," *Issues in Science and Technology*, Winter 2010.

Ian Sample, "Warmer Atlantic Fuels Hurricanes, UK Study Finds," *Guardian*, January 31, 2008.

Quirin Schiermeier, "Glacier Estimate Is on Thin Ice: IPCC May Modify Its Himalayan Melting Forecasts," *Nature*, January 21, 2010.

Peter H. Wyckoff and Rachel Bowers, "Response of the Prairie-Forest Border to Climate Change: Impacts of Increasing Drought May Be Mitigated by Increasing CO_2," *Journal of Ecology*, January 2010.

Internet Sources

American Institute of Physics, "The Discovery of Global Warming," July 2009.

Climate Progress, "Drought in Southern Australia Declared 'Worst on Record,'" October 10, 2008. http://climateprogress .org.

Environmental Protection Agency, "Recent Climate Change," September 28, 2009. www.epa.gov.

The Heat Is Online, "Extreme Weather Profile: January–June, 2010." www.heatisonline.org.

Intergovernmental Panel on Climate Change, "Climate Change 2007: Synthesis Report." www.ipcc.ch.

The National Academies Press, "Global Climate Change and Extreme Weather Events: Understanding the Contributions to Infectious Disease Emergence," n.d. www.nap.edu.

National Oceanic and Atmospheric Administration, "Billion Dollar U.S. Weather Disasters," n.d. http://lwf.ncdc.noaa.gov.

National Wildlife Federation, "Global Warming Bringing More Oddball Winter Weather," January 28, 2010. www.nwf.org.

Nova Online, "Tracking El Niño," January, 1998. www.pbs.org.

Web Sites

Intergovernmental Panel on Climate Change (www.ipcc.ch). The United Nations and World Meteorological Organization–sponsored panel of scientists that is responsible for assessing the scientific, technical, and socioeconomic information relevant to the understanding of climate change.

Marian Koshland Science Museum of the National Academy of Sciences (www.koshland-science-museum.org/exhibitgcc). This site presents an authoritative survey of global warming issues in a series of straightforward and well-organized pages.

New Scientist: Climate Change (www.newscientist.com/topic/ climate-change). A page dedicated to the topic of climate change, carrying a wealth of articles on current developments in the field.

Pew Center on Global Climate Change (www.pewclimate.org). A nonprofit organization undertaking scientific investigation of the global warming issue, as well as business and governmental policy analysis on the economic and social challenges of climate change.

United Nations Environment Programme (www.unep.org/ climatechange). Web site operated by the United Nations' umbrella group for environmental issues, which includes the Intergovernmental Panel on Climate Change.

University of Copenhagen: Climate Change (http://climatecon gress.ku.dk). A site offering information and reports originating with the UN Conference on Climate Change, held in Copenhagen in 2009.

Index

About the Author

Tom Streissguth has authored more than one hundred books of nonfiction for the school and library market. He specializes in biography, history, geography, and current-affairs topics. For the Gale Group, he has recently completed *The Greenhaven Encyclopedia of the Renaissance*, a comprehensive guide to the artists, scientists, culture, and major events of this formative time in European history. A graduate of Yale University, he has worked as an editor, teacher, and author and currently lives in Minnesota.

✓checkouts - 12/13/22)